TOM GRAVES

WHITE BOY

A Memoir

ADVANCE READER COPY

DEVAULT-GRAVES
DIGITAL EDITIONS

Print book ISBN: 978-1-942531-31-9
eBook ISBN: 978-1-942531-32-6

Cover design: Martina Voriskova and Patrick Alley
Layout: Patrick Alley
Front cover photograph: Tom Graves, 1st grade school photograph

DEVAULT-GRAVES
DIGITAL EDITIONS
www.devault-gravesagency.com

Devault-Graves Digital Editions is an imprint of
The Devault-Graves Agency, LLC,
Memphis, Tennessee.
The names Devault-Graves Digital Editions, Lasso Books,
and Chalk Line Books are all imprints and
trademarks of The Devault-Graves Agency, LLC.
www.devault-gravesagency.com

Other Books by Tom Graves

Fiction

Pullers

Aesop's Fables with Colin Hay (audiobook)

Nonfiction

Crossroads: The Life and Afterlife of Blues Legend Robert Johnson
*winner of the Keeping the Blues Alive Award

Louise Brooks, Frank Zappa, & Other Charmers & Dreamers

Graceland Too Revisited
(photography with Darrin Devault)

Table of Contents

Author's Note

For the sake of protecting the privacy of some of the people named in this memoir who are still living, I have changed or altered names. In every other respect, however, this is a true account.

Drinking Out of the Colored Fountain

I AM FROM A racist family. I was educated in a racist school. I was a parishioner in a racist church. I live in a racist city.

This being Memphis, however, the racism is complex, ironic, and like Einstein's concept of time seems to fold in on itself. In my childhood the world seemed to be divided two ways: by gender and by race. There were men and there were women, and there were white people and there were black people. And that was all there was to it. I was only vaguely aware that there were others who fell outside those parameters. This state of affairs seemed logical to me. God created man and woman and he intended for them to have children, to be fruitful and multiply as the book said. People grew up, got old, died, and went to heaven, or if they were bad to that other place. And for reasons we didn't really understand, he created white people to show black people how they should properly live. That white people were superior to black people didn't even need suggestion. That fact—along with the word "nigger"—was in the very air we breathed in Memphis in the '50s and '60s.

There were restrooms for girls and restrooms for boys.

There were restrooms clearly marked for whites and those clearly marked for "coloreds," which was the polite way in that time to refer to niggers. I knew those signs and obeyed them long before I hit first grade in 1960 and learned to read. There were also water fountains with the delineations "white" and "colored" and we were told not to drink out of *their* water fountains. Somewhere in the celluloid haze of films I have watched over the years, I remember a scene of a black boy drinking out of the colored fountain and he glances around to see if anyone is looking and steals a sip from the white fountain. I'm here to tell you that white children, myself most certainly included, did the same thing in reverse, drinking out of the colored fountain when no one, especially our parents, was looking. To my surprise, the water did not taste different.

I was born in 1954, and because I'm either blessed or cursed with a very vivid and accurate memory of my childhood, can remember the racial divisions in the South with crystal clarity. I remember how, as my family traveled to their birthplace in Pine Bluff, Arkansas to visit their kinfolk every few months, we would beg to stop at an ice cream stand in Clarendon, Arkansas on every trip. Whites ordered from one side of the building and blacks ordered from the other side. I do not remember that any signs were posted. That was just the way things were and everybody in the small town knew the drill.

I also remember that the Memphis Zoo, one of my favorite places, had one day per week, Thursday it has been confirmed, reserved exclusively for blacks. Nigger Day as we called it in those unenlightened times. The late Ernest Withers, the great African-American photographer from Memphis who was a friend of mine, has a justifiably famous photo of a sign posted outside the zoo that says "No White People Allowed In Zoo Today" with a background of black Memphians blithely walking beyond the gates, no whites in sight, and a black woman sitting on the sign. There was also a Nigger Day at the Fairgrounds Amusement Park.

One of my first inklings that something wasn't right with the black and white equation was when our family was picnicking with some old family friends who were visiting from Florida. There was discussion of everyone meeting again at the zoo in a few days.

I tugged at my Dad's sleeve and whispered, "Dad, we can't go on that day. That's Nigger Day."

My Dad was a fair man despite his racist leanings. Without fail he rooted for the underdog in almost any given situation and even though he had what the Graves family referred to as the Graves temper, I never heard him say a cross thing to anyone in day-to-day life, whether white or black. Now, if someone was giving him some grief or a hard time, like the comic book hero the Human Torch he could turn his flame on. He brooked no nonsense. Yet I cannot imagine him giving away candy treats to a group of children—he loved kids—and not making sure the black kids got an equal number of candies as the white kids. That just wasn't in his nature.

But just let him read the headlines in the local paper about integration or civil rights or a protest downtown and black thunderclouds would form over his head and his ire and dismay would find form in long monologues at the dinner table, monologues at least until I was old enough to start questioning some of his ideas and then dinnertime became a verbal sparring match.

When I told Dad we couldn't visit the zoo on that particular day he replied, "Son, they can't go on our days, but we can go on theirs."

Even at five or six years old, this struck me as a queer deal indeed. "They can't go on *our* days but we can go on *theirs*."

This wasn't the first clue that something was wrong. The first would have to be singing that Sunday School mainstay, "Jesus Loves the Little Children." The song specified that Jesus loved them one and all equally, "red and yellow, black and white, they are precious in his sight." The illustrations that accompanied the song sheet in our Sunday School books showed a very Caucasian Jesus surrounded by children of all races. The message of equality was quite clear, even in a church that was lily-white.

So, if Jesus, who I had been taught from birth was my

Lord and Savior, the one I said my prayers to every night when I went to bed, saw no difference between black children and white children, then why did they live over in Niggertown, which was demonstrably poorer and shabbier than the white parts of Memphis, and why did they have their own churches and their own histrionic manner of worship and we couldn't be friends with them? Why were there separate restrooms, water fountains, places to sit in the movie theater, seats on the bus, kitchen entrances at restaurants, separate waiting rooms at the doctor's office?

I didn't understand these things. To further confuse matters, black and white children played in harmony on *The Little Rascals* film shorts shown weekdays on local television. Renamed from the 1930s Hal Roach *Our Gang* two-reelers, these films were not only hilarious but showed that some of the black kids, Stymie in particular, were more clever than most of their white counterparts. One scene I recall was when an evil white step-mother gave her spoiled son bacon and eggs for breakfast and made her step-children eat mush, which sounded dreadful. Stymie tricked the spoiled son into fixing all of them a king-sized bacon and eggs breakfast.

Amos 'n' Andy played on Memphis television every afternoon for years. The show is vilified today by many African-Americans for racial stereotyping and is further tarred by the now long-ago memory of the hit radio show that spawned the television series that was done in blackface and "Negro" dialect by two white comedians. While I do understand those misgivings, there is still some complexity there for me. My father was a fleet mechanic for the Bell Telephone Company, a good-paying union job that fed and clothed a family of four and provided a tidy little thousand square-foot home with a tidy little mortgage.

Unlike Amos and the Kingfish, my folks never went to fancy restaurants. Until I turned 18, the fanciest restaurant I had ever been in was Britling Cafeteria in Memphis, which was dazzling enough to me. I couldn't imagine my parents in a place as opulent as those where Andy and the Kingfish would routinely create mayhem, or my father being outfitted at a tailor's for a suit, or being a member of a lodge. Those things were for rich people, and the TV show of *Amos'n' Andy* showed a lot of what, to me, was rich black folks.

My parents were very strict about my brother and me saying "yes ma'am" and "no ma'am," "yes sir" and "no sir" to anyone of adult age. It was unthinkable for us to call any grown-up by his or her first name. Except in the case of blacks. The church janitor and his wife, who I write about in this book, were known to us as Ed and Ophelia. The white custodian of my elementary school, Bethel Grove, was Mr. Fox. His helper, the janitor, was known simply as Charlie and I said hello to him every school day.

One day I asked my father if I was supposed to say "yes sir" and "no sir" to blacks (that's not the word I used, I'm afraid). This question caught Dad by surprise.

He thought about it for a good minute then said, "Well, I don't guess it would hurt anything." Then a heartbeat later he added, "But they don't have to force you to."

My Dad, who was nice to pretty much everyone, hated black people. No question or guessing about it. When I was older and things in our culture began to gradually change, my Dad would still drop the N-word around new company just to gauge the reaction. Generally, there was no reaction, especially if the company in question shared the rural Southern roots of my parents or were from the blue collar class. I began to get more and more uneasy about this habit of his, especially when the company was more mixed and we were around a politer set. From a very early age I understood class differences; that the wealthier you were then the better you spoke, the more refinement you displayed, the better you dressed, the bigger your house was. And you didn't say *that* word. This was completely reinforced on television. Robert Young in *Father Knows Best* came home from work every day wearing a suit and tie and changed into an evening jacket. My dad came home from work smudged with grease in a sweat-stained uniform, the same as most of the other dads I knew. But I could see with my own two eyes that there was a bigger, more rarified world out there, a world where people knew the right fork to use, the proper words to speak, and that if you were good in school and studied hard you too could be one of those people.

Right from the first grade I developed at least three ways of talking. There was proper language in school. Talk at home where I could say "ain't." And talk in rural Arkansas where the rules of grammar were thrown right out the school window. Curiously, neither of my parents spoke with a heavy Southern accent. Although at a young age I could speak with grammatical precision, I had and have retained a pronounced Memphis brogue, kind of like Elvis, if you will. But even that has changed.

At a high school reunion a few years back a former class-mate with an accent as thick as overcooked grits said, "Tommy, why don't you talk *lak* you used to?"

When I brought home my first As in first grade, my parents began to talk up me going to college. It was understood by all of us that I would be the first college graduate in our large extended family, the example, and I was. I took to reading very quickly and would read practically anything I could get my hands on. Wanting to nurture my intellectual curiosity, Mom and Dad bought an expensive set of *World Book* encyclopedias. I remember the day they arrived. I had my Mom look up about a thousand things—Mom is there one on "octopus?" Is there one on "rhinoceroses?" On "dinosaurs?" Those books served me well even after I had made it to college.

By second grade I had discovered the solar system and its planets. I was fascinated, enthralled. There was a class rule that we had to check out and read a book from our school library every week. Before long I had read almost every book in the second grade section. I particularly loved the Cowboy Sam books. And then I began to stray from the second grade stack into places in the library I wasn't supposed to go. I found a book on the planets in the fifth grade section. When I showed the book to my teacher for approval she told me the book was at a higher level than I could read, that it would be beyond me. As the class lined up to leave, I still did not have a book. The teacher told me to get a book quickly and come on back to the classroom when I was done. Well, me being me, I checked out the forbidden fifth grade book and got a thorough scolding when I returned to class with it.

At the end of the week we were supposed to give a book report in front of the class. Well, I knew all about the planets by this time and I sure as heck was going to tell my classmates everything I knew about them. I did so with my customary zeal and brio and not only won over my classmates, but the teacher as well.

Afterwards she told me I could check out any book I wanted.

The Graves Family

MY FATHER'S FAMILY WAS far more racist than my mother's side, the Rogers. Use of the N-word didn't change that much between families, but the attitude most certainly did. My Dad took the race issue dead seriously. He did not tell nigger jokes. My mom did. Her mother did. Her father, my granddad, although without much formal education, was highly intelligent, skilled, mild-mannered, and more racially sensitive. He had been a foreman on different plantations in the Arkansas Delta and was much respected by the workers, especially the blacks, for his fair hand. Later he was a foreman at the top secret Pine Bluff Arsenal, a highly classified military installation, and won awards for some of his innovative ideas (I have no idea what these ideas were) and praise for his management skills with laborers at the arsenal.

Granddad lived down a gravel road out in the country and during pleasant weather we would sit outdoors in metal lawn chairs where I was well-schooled in the art of Southern storytelling. Every now and then an elderly black man or woman would slowly amble by the house down the gravel road and my grandfather in loud voice would greet them and they would always greet him in return. Even though I had never seen their homes, I knew that blacks lived in patches all up and down the road. I never heard an unkind word spoken about them.

One visit, as I entered my grandparents' house, I saw a black teenaged girl ironing clothes in the living room. I had never seen her there before.

"Who is that?" I whispered to my grandmother.

"Oh that's Margie. She's does ironing for me sometimes. Don't y'all act up around her."

So why was my father and his family so stridently racist? The answers haven't been easy to find, and I have certainly asked. I have some clues, however. My grandfather on the Graves' side, John Graves, was a tall, strong, humorless authoritarian who had raised a family of six children when his first wife died. In his fifties he married my much younger grandmother, Mattie Poynter, and began a second family that would total seven more children. There were two boys in this new family followed by my father and his twin sister, my Aunt Rachel, who at 94 years old I consulted about the family's attitudes about race. Then there was a second set of twins, boys, and late in the game, my Uncle Norman, who is still very much alive today. In the 1920s my grandfather was a foreman in a local lumber mill and made good money. The family moved from the city of Pine Bluff out to the country where the expanding family would have room to breathe and run free. My father had been wet-nursed by a black woman and she foretold that my dad was going to be the sickly one. Out of this large family it was borne out; my father was the first of his siblings to die, at the age of 57, of lung cancer caused by cigarette smoking, which he had picked up in combat in World War II.

When the Graves family moved out to the country, Sulphur Springs it was called, they brought a black nanny, Aunt Littie, with them. There was apparently some sort of social taboo against blacks living in the same house as whites, so a house nearly identical to the family home was built behind the family house especially for Aunt Littie, although virtually all of her day was spent in the family home tending to the Graves' business.

My Aunt Rachel today says about Aunt Littie, "We just adored her. She was definitely one of the family. She had her own little house to live in and helped Momma do the cooking and cleaning and all the taking care of kids. We loved her like one of our own."

I do not doubt this. This is a refrain I've heard all my life in the South. People who hate blacks as a group but genuinely love specific blacks they know.

It is easier to hate the enemy you do not know than the one you do.

*   *   *

Not long ago, I discovered in my parents' effects a photograph of the Graves family, slightly faded and out of focus enough to make me think this must have been taken with an early Brownie camera. My grandfather, John Graves, the patriarch, stands in the middle of his brood, and my grandmother, Mattie, stands solemnly beside him. My grandfather is wearing an open-necked shirt with a suit and a hat that is tilted at a stylish angle. My Uncle Richard, the eldest child, is wearing a tie. The other children are lined-up in front of their parents. A nice tricycle is in the foreground, testimony to a good job and a good salary. Standing proudly behind my Uncle Richard is Aunt Littie, who appears to be in her fifties or sixties, wearing a polka dot dress that comes nearly to her ankles and a head wrap. She is of stout physique.

According to family lore, when she got too old to care for the children any longer, she was placed back in town with her kinfolk. What I'd bet really happened is that the Graves family was left penniless by the Great Depression and could not afford even the small salary Aunt Littie was undoubtedly paid. John Graves lost his job at the lumber mill when it burned down in the 1930s and never again in his lifetime was to find steady work. He was offered at least one other lumber mill job in the Pacific Northwest and for reasons I do not know or understand refused it. Perhaps he simply did not want to give up his homestead in Pine Bluff, which in my estimation was a poor decision.

So John Graves and his family languished in poverty—often dire poverty—for the entire next decade, truck farming, scraping by, until World War II took every one of his sons away to war except the youngest, Norman, who was not of draft age. A rule in effect during the War was that at least one son would be left behind on family farms. The Pine Bluff draft board dismissed my father's protestations that he was the last son to help out on the family farm, probably thinking a leached-out patch of dirt in Sulphur Springs didn't amount to any kind of real farm, and shipped him off to the Pacific Theater, where he fought in the battles of Leyte and Mindanao in the Philippines, horror shows both. Dad was bitter the rest of his life and at times sounded scarily like the cynical, half-demented character Sgt. Welsh in James Jones' *The Thin Red Line*.

My dad harbored yet another grudge against blacks because he heard a couple of them grousing about receiving combat duty as punishment. They had been kitchen workers, but due to some kind of infractions were sent to the front, which to them was like a death sentence. My father felt that if it was his duty to fight, why wasn't it theirs? How did they have a right to complain and he didn't? Because he didn't like what these two men had to say, he transposed it to *all* black men. They *all* became shirkers. They *all* became draft dodgers.

The Graves Brothers in uniform right after World War II. From left, my father, Raymond Lee Graves, Harry Graves, Roland Graves, Harold Graves, and Richard Graves. You wouldn't want to mess with them.

The Graves family had a reputation in the Pine Bluff area for very tough men who countenanced no insult or wrong, and who were vain and prideful. They accepted no charity and woe be unto anyone who treated them as if they were poor, which they most certainly were. People like the Graves were often denegrated by higher-ups as "white niggers." There is no doubt in my mind that in the corners of the schoolyard they heard that epithet leveled at them. They were as poor as the destitute blacks who populated the Deep South during the Depression and they knew it. When you are down that low and you feel the scorn of others, you seek to find somebody lower, someone you can cast your own hatreds on.

The Graves family was Methodist. Once a month, the Knights of the Ku Klux Klan, who were a power throughout much of the nation in the 1920s, would file onto the back row of the Methodist Church in Watson Chapel in full hoods and sheets, their faces hidden. No one knew who the Klansmen were, supposedly, but you can bet a lot of guesswork was going on. The Graves boys looked at all the Klansmen's hands and knew by the set of strong, callused, scarred hands that their father was sitting among them. I had been told that my grandfather occasionally "rode" with the Klan, but only recently did I learn he was in fact a sheet-wearing, cross-burning, night-riding Klansman. Which explains a lot about why the Graves family was so much more racist than my Mom's Rogers side of the family.

The Klan's stranglehold in Pine Bluff lasted well into the 1970s when I was to actually witness a Ku Klux Klan rally. Circa 1972 I was riding in a car with my cousin Richard Graves, who I will always call Rick. Rick this past year retired as a Lutheran chaplain and major in the U.S. Army. In those days, however, Rick had shoulder-length auburn hair and played bass guitar in a succession of rock bands. His bandmates were with us during this night and we passed a baseball field I had seen many, many times in my family's frequent visits to Pine Bluff. I was beyond shocked to see a flock of white-sheeted Klansmen in the field gathering around an electric, not a burning, cross. The lightbulbs were red. Also the Klansmen did not have their face masks down to cover their faces.

My cousin and his bandmates were used to Klan rallies and didn't think much of it. It certainly got my attention, however. I later learned that a billboard in Pine Bluff that had been up for years that showed a photograph of Martin Luther

King Jr. in a classroom with the bold headline "Martin Luther King Jr. in Communist Training Class" was funded by both the Klan and the White Citizens' Council of Pine Bluff. My paternal grandmother's brother, Uncle Don, was president of that chapter of the White Citizens' Council. For much of my young life I couldn't understand how black people could lionize a man who was a known Communist. By the time I was 14 and Dr. King was assassinated on the streets of Memphis, I had learned what racist propaganda was.

This same cousin, Rick, has always been the family member most interested in the Graves' genealogy. We had always heard and believed that our family was Scots-Irish and that certainly seemed to fit the history of that region of Arkansas. Most of the working class Southerners in that part of the state were Scots-Irish, fiercely protestant, fiercely supremacist, and fiercely loyal to whatever the cause. Most Klansmen in the South were of Scots-Irish ancestry. The plantation class, such as those who owned the rich, alluvial farmland in the Mississippi Delta, was nearly always of British descent and looked down on the white trash who were the Scots-Irish.

Rick sent off his DNA to be analyzed and to trace back our family tree. What he found out was startling to the whole family. We weren't Scots-Irish after all. We were Brits. Our lineage goes directly back to the Jamestown Colony and to a captain Thomas Graves, a "gentleman" who arrived on the second supply to Jamestown in 1608. Thomas Graves was a fortune hunter who wanted to see what financial opportunities might await him in the New World. After seeing where the money was to be made, Graves returned to England to secure financing. During this time much of the Jamestown Colony was decimated due to mass starvation. Upon the return of Graves and other new settlers, he was eventually appointed captain and lived out the remainder of his life in Virginia.

For 200 years the Graves family gained wealth and prominence according to historical record. Apparently the Graveses owned plantations and it is almost certain that they owned slaves. Then the record is obscured. We aren't certain what happened, but it seems that the Civil War ruined the fortunes of the Graves family, who did not recover in any appreciable way until after the Second World War. With a decline in fortunes, when one people is set free and another brought to its knees, you are almost certain to have an irrational, burning, reason-retardant hatred that brews through family and years.

The Graveses, a proud family of British gentlemen, were reduced to ashes and white sheets in the aftermath of their undoing.

For the first part of my life I seldom questioned my racist upbringing even as I squirmed when Dad would spit out the N-word in mixed company. After all, just about everyone else did the same thing.

Then something strange and terrible happened. I actually got to know some black people. And my world turned.

Ophelia (A Memory)

MY EARLIEST MEMORY TOOK eleven years to come to me. It happened when I was in the sixth grade, about eleven years old. That was the year my grade school, Bethel Grove, integrated a significantly large group of black students. The previous year the school hesitantly dipped their toes into those troubled racial waters by bringing precisely one little black girl to Bethel Grove. Her name was Andrea.

I discovered that Bethel Grove had been silently integrated that school year when, on the first day of class, I walked past the classroom windows and glancing inside noticed a solitary, tidy, well-groomed black child sitting erect at her desk, perfect posture, wearing a pair of cat's eye glasses. My first thought was one of shock. *They* are in our school! I dreaded telling my father because I knew he would fume and make our lives at home miserable at the dinner table. His favorite topic for the remainder of his life was how black people were ruining things for us whites.

My second and more lingering thought was that this little black girl had to be the loneliest person in the whole world, sitting there all by herself. No friends her own color to laugh and play with.

The sky did not fall. The ground did not shake.

Dad grumbled and said, "I knew this was going to happen," and left to fume about something else.

Only a handful of parents transferred their children to other schools, where they were faced with the same dilemma all over again. After a few days no one much mentioned Andrea any longer. Life had moved on. The only difference was less use of the N-word on the playground and no use of it at all in the classroom, where formerly the word had been quietly tolerated.

Obviously the stealth integration of one black child at Bethel Grove had been well orchestrated by the school board to minimize white panic and over-reaction. The following year, 1965, the *real* integration began, with at least 30 percent of the Bethel Grove student population black, the kids coming from the southern portion of the notorious Orange Mound neighborhood, which was located on the other side of Lamar Avenue that for decades had served as a line of demarcation separating blacks and whites.

By 1965 everyone had seen this coming. The only escape for whites so inclined was to send their kids to a private school, which cost money, much more than the average blue collar family from the Bethel Grove neighborhood could afford. So everyone bit down hard and swallowed integration. There were no fights between blacks and whites in the schoolyard. The black kids did not bring switchblade knives and razors as we had feared. And about the reports of uncleanliness and poor hygiene, those kids were better groomed than we were.

The principal, Miss Pittman, had one little trick left up her sleeve. I have no way of proving this was a calculated maneuver on her part, but my gut feeling is that it was. She created a split-level class, half fifth graders, half sixth graders. This was an accelerated class, reserved for the best and brightest students. My belief is that Miss Pittman did this both to protect the smarter white kids from the perceived coarsening effect of lower class black students and to give the brighter black students a chance at higher achievement.

I was selected for the sixth grade side of the classroom, one of 12 sixth graders. Two black students, Joyce and Sharon, were in my sixth grade section. Two were in the fifth grade section as well: Andrea, the little girl who all by herself had integrated Bethel Grove the previous year, and Catherine, a skinny little thing in pigtails whose backwoods accent was so impenetrable that we often couldn't understand a word she was saying. Catherine's accent was so bad that our teacher, Miss Dinkins, sent her to the school's speech therapist. My memory of Andrea and Catherine is that they rarely uttered a word. Sharon and Joyce, on the other hand, were much more loquacious, especially Sharon, who loved to braid the white girls' hair.

The first grade teachers at Bethel Grove, including my beloved first grade teacher, Mrs. Stevens, were getting up in age and were finding teaching calisthenics to the children during recess too taxing. Also, one of the teachers was pregnant and most certainly not capable of jumping jacks and push-ups. The solution was to get the boys from the accelerated sixth grade class to lead the first graders in their exercises.

This meant we would have to give up our own recess

period, but duty called and I was assigned to Mrs. Stevens' class, reuniting me with the teacher I loved the most. I wasn't prepared for the reception we got from the first graders. They were overjoyed to have us among them.

Children that age do not see color. They do not see race. They would practically fight each other over who would get to hold our hands as we formed a circle or a line for Red Rover games. My first memory came to me when a happy, giggling, precious little black girl pushed her way to be first to hold my hand. As soon as she touched me an alarm bell clanged in my head: you are touching a *nigger!* I had never touched a black person in my life. Or so I thought at that particular moment. I'm happy to report that as soon as that thought whistled into my brain it vanished as soon as I saw the look of utter joy on that little girl's face. Never again would I quail at the touch of a black person or have a moment's hesitation holding a black child's hand or giving one a needed hug. This one act on this one day broke a thousand taboos I had been pinioned with during my first eleven years of life.

And it gave me my earliest memory back. When that little girl touched my hand the most wonderful memory of Ophelia came sailing back to me. Ophelia was the older black woman who tended babies in the nursery at Charjean Baptist Church where my parents were members. My parents were not social people as such, and what little social world they had typically revolved around the church. Soon after birth, I was bottle fed, coddled, and soothed by Ophelia on Sundays. I remembered her calming voice, her pleasing smell, her starched nurse's uniform, and most of all the comfort of her touch. That little girl holding my hand brought me back to Ophelia.

As I had grown, even while in the sixth grade, I would stop and say hello to Ophelia and her husband, Ed, who was the church janitor and was well-liked enough that he was permitted to smoke his cigars—which he always put in a cigar holder when he smoked them that I always thought was a touch of class—in the back of the church away from the sanctuary. My mom told me that Ophelia took a special shine to my brother Norris when he was a baby, telling people "that one's mine." The very mention of Ophelia's name brings back not so much a flood of memories, but a flood of *feelings*. All of them warm and good and a balm for my spirit.

Through the magic of Facebook I put out some inquiries about Ophelia. No one could tell me what had happened to her. Surely she would now be dead and it bothers me that I can't visit her gravesite or know who her folks are so I could call them to reminisce. One person who is my exact same age, Buster Sterling, remembered Ophelia babysitting him. His mother was the secretary for Charjean Baptist Church and hired Ophelia often to babysit and to do small household chores. Buster remembered her ironing clothes and humming as she worked.

All it took was the touch of one little girl to remind me of Ophelia. That touch meant everything.

And then there is the kind of touch that can cause you trouble. As I mentioned, I was in an accelerated split-level class—one half was fifth grade, the other sixth grade. I was sheltered from the greater mass of incoming black students that year. This was the first time that most of us white kids ever interacted in any substantial way with fellow blacks. Going from an all-white social structure to one in which we were expected to learn together, play together, eat together, and socialize together was a giant leap considering that these were a people we had been taught from birth to look down on as inferiors.

Considering the social gamble involved, the strategy succeeded surprisingly well. As stated, there weren't fistfights or shivs secreted in boots to cut us with, and the simple truth is a lot of these black kids were loads of fun. But leave it to me to discover the kink in the armor.

As I was exiting the boys' restroom one school day a black boy from the fifth grade who I didn't know stopped me and said, "Boy, did you touch that bathroom do' on your way out?"

This confused me. "Sure, yeah, I touched the door. What's the matter?"

"Boy, don't you touch that bathroom do' no mo'," he commanded with menace. "If I catch you touching that bathroom do' ag'in I'm gonna whup yo' ass."

And then he walked off like he owned the building.

This shocked me to my core. To me he looked tough enough to carry out his threat. Even though he was in a lower grade he was my size and everyone knew the Negro race were nothing but walking death squads. I was terrified.

What to do? I certainly wasn't going to challenge him. I had enough chicken in my DNA to prevent that from happening. I didn't dare tell my teacher or go to the principal because, as you will read later, I had learned my lesson about telling on people. And if I got him in trouble he might tell his gang and they'd cut my throat after school.

I knew better than tell my Dad. My family protected Dad from himself, because when he lost his temper he lost his good sense. I had no idea what he might do if he thought I were being picked on by a black bully. So I kept mum on the subject and held my fear inside.

Every day at school I scouted the halls for this boy and when the coast was clear I'd dash into the bathroom, take care of business, and dash out as quickly as possible. I also held it as much as I could, waiting when possible to urinate at home. This seemed like a good plan and thus far it had worked.

Then one day when all seemed safe I sped out the door and nearly ran smack into my antagonist as I rounded a corner. Caught off guard, I just waved and said "hi!" thinking he'd let his threat pass, just maybe.

"Boy, did you touch that do' when you left that bathroom? I told you I'd whup yo' ass if you touched that do'."

What happened next has only happened to me a couple of times in my entire life.

Instead of flight—running like hell—I summoned the ghosts of the graybeards from my past, some of whom were king-hell badasses, brought myself up to full height and said, "Of course I touched that damn door. How am I supposed to pee if I don't go in the bathroom? I touched that door and I'm gonna keep touching the door and there's not a damn thing you're gonna do about it."

Then I prepared to die.

He gave me a quizzical look, stuck out his hand and said, "Man, you my best friend. You can touch that do' anytime you want."

And that's how Joe and I became friends.

*   *   *

One of the great pleasures of my youth was hanging out at my school playground during summer break. The Memphis Park Commission employed one male and one female college student to serve during those summers as park commissioners and they guided us in all manner of sports, recreation, and arts and crafts in their starched all-white uniforms. We universally adored our park commissioners and never let the brutal Memphis heat interfere with a sweaty good time.

For our amusement there was a tetherball pole (a teen boy with one arm slaughtered all competition at this game), a box hockey box where ferocious matches were held, volleyball, tennis, softball, track, touch football, etc. Also there was a sandbox that contained enough cat doo to keep most of us clear of it.

After breakfast, I usually walked or rode my bicycle one block north of Boyle Avenue to the Bethel Grove playground where the fun would begin.

One morning during the 1965-66 school year as I dismounted from my bicycle a playmate came up to me and said, "Did you hear what happened yesterday?"

"No," I replied, "what happened?"

"A little nigger boy rode his bicycle over here and got off to play in the sandbox. The old man across the street over there saw the little nigger boy playing and came over and cussed the boy out and told him to get back to Niggertown where he belonged."

About midway into the discussion our park commissioner, who I remember was named Mike Miles, overheard the tail-end of the conversation and asked us to repeat exactly what happened. My playmate obliged with a full and colorful description.

"He can't do that," Miles angrily told us regarding the old man's behavior. "He has no right whatsoever to tell anyone, black or white, that they can't play on this playground. This playground is open to everyone no matter who they are. I'm going to have a word with him."

He marched straight across the street and knocked firmly on the old man's door. We looked on aghast because we knew what a mean old troll this man was. He was the type who would holler at children to "get off my grass." We were all scared to death of him.

The old man peered out his door at the handsome young man dressed in his all-white starched uniform. We couldn't hear exactly what was being said but judging from the body language Mike Miles was setting the old man straight and the old man, looking guilty as hell, nodded in agreement apparently understanding he was in the wrong and had better not do it again.

Mike Miles strode back across the street, standing tall, with an air of righteousness in his step.

As he passed us by he said, "Well, I told that son of a gun."

We never saw that black kid again.

Who's Chicken?

AS PREVIOUSLY MENTIONED, I was in an accelerated sixth grade class that had two African-American girls who I distinctly remember today. Their names were Joyce and Sharon. Unlike Joyce, Sharon was not one bit shy and was quite a talker. She was not intimidated by being in a nearly all-white class. Including me, there were six boys in this class, all of whom were white.

One day one of the boys said to me, "I dare you to ask Sharon if she's an Ethiopian."

I was quick to take a dare and my fellow student knew it. I would have never taunted either Joyce or Sharon with those racist words we all know. I am not a cruel person and by nature I do not enjoy hurting people's feelings. However, I knew that Ethiopia was an African nation and I knew that this would be a mild slight against Sharon, but in my arrogance and ignorance I truly thought that Sharon would be too dim to know what Ethiopia was.

"Hey Sharon, are you an Ethiopian?" I asked deadpan.

She fixed a look on me that could have guided missiles.

"Ha-ha Tommy Graves. *Very* funny."

And she kept on staring.

In a very, very low voice I croaked out, "I'm sorry. Just kidding."

I could feel the crimson heat in my face. I slunk down in my chair and hoped to God she wouldn't tell on me.

Another day in my sixth grade class I asked the other students if they had seen a mule-driven wagon the previous day that rolled down my street. This was in the 1965-66 school year and these were the last years in which on rare occasion some older black farmers from South Memphis would hitch up their mule-driven old wagons and drive them down our street on the way to a farmers' market about a mile away. We could hear the cloppity-clop of the mules and the driver loudly calling out to them from blocks away and it was a novel enough occurrence that we would stop our play and wait to greet the old farmers as they passed and wave at them.

No one else happened to have seen this particular farmer and his mules, but the conversation steered onto farms and farm animals. My grandfather on my mother's side, Clarence Rogers, kept a small farmyard when I was a youth so I was used to cows, chickens, pigs, and other farm animals. I knew enough not to ever cross a fence where there was a bull, and to stay far away from a sow with her piglets. I wasn't so fortunate when I tangled with what I had been warned was a "bad" rooster. My whole young life I had chased chickens just for the fun of it—all boys do—and it was inconceivable to me that a rooster was capable of any kind of violence toward me at all.

So I caught that rooster unawares and chased him into a culvert where he was cornered.

"Ha-ha, I won," I congratulated myself and turned to walk away.

All of a sudden I felt claws digging into my back and wings flapping about my head. I tore out of that culvert screaming to high heaven in full view of my Granddad and my uncle, the rooster beating my back half to death with his wings. I ran at least a hundred yards at warp speed before the rooster decided he had taught me my lesson and went back to his hens. Until the day he died, Granddaddy never tired of telling anyone who would listen how I had met my match with his rooster.

I told the story of my showdown with the rooster which provoked great laughter among my classmates. Joyce, the quieter of the two black girls in my sixth grade section, mentioned that she had never seen a chicken. Not in real life, anyway. This absolutely stunned me. I could not imagine *anyone* having not seen a chicken.

I asked her, "You've never been to a farm before?"

"Nope."

"You never went to the Fair where they have the chickens and cows?"

"Nope."

This both perplexed and saddened me. This just wasn't right, I thought to myself. *Everybody* needs to know what a doggone chicken looks like. This made me realize just how homebound and neighborhood-bound many of these black children were. Many of them had never traveled more than a few miles from their neighborhoods. There were many Mississippi transplants among black Memphians. The blues songs so familiar to those in the Mid-South were filled with barnyard references ("The Little Red Rooster," for instance.) But there were just as many who hadn't left Memphis for several generations.

Right then I decided I needed to hatch a plan for Joyce and any others in our class who hadn't ever visited the country to go with our family to Arkansas to my grandparents' place out in the country where they could see real farm animals. I thought of how we could all cram into the backseat of my parents' '58 Buick and how we could all sleep on the floor in my grandparents' living room. And my Grandmama could fix us all a whopping great big country breakfast with the best biscuits in the whole world.

I am a hatcher of plans. I've been like Mickey Rooney as Andy Hardy my whole life. Full of ideas and enthusiasm. *"Let's put on a show!"* But the other shoe always drops. On my way home from school I began to think of the social logistics of getting Dad and my grandparents to host black kids on such an excursion. Eating together? That was a maybe. Sleeping together in one or even two rooms? No way. Plus getting permission from Joyce's parents to take her 160 miles into the Jim Crow South with white folks. No, that might not work either.

As we sat down to our family dinner that evening, my brain was racing. How could I make this work? Finally, I spoke up.

"Daddy, guess what? The colored girl in my class, Joyce, said she'd never seen a real chicken before. What do you think of that?"

"Ain't that somethin'?"

"I wish she could see some of Granddaddy's chickens."

"Yeah, that'd be nice. I guess she's never done any traveling out of Memphis."

"Nossir, I guess not."

And that's precisely where we left it. I couldn't count the times in the 50-plus years since that day that I haven't thought about Joyce and wanting to take her with us to Arkansas. After that school year we moved to the all-white suburbs of Parkway Village. I never saw Joyce again nor did I ever hear another word about her. Joyce, and Sharon too, are now lost to time.

Maybe it was the thought that counted.

Who You Is?

AT THE URGING OF a friend, I spat into a plastic tube and mailed the spittle off to 23andMe, a company that analyzes DNA. Until recently I had not been that interested in my genealogy. One reason for my lack of interest is because I knew that my great-grandfather on my paternal grandmother's side fought in the Confederacy. This would be Robert Harrison Poynter who later became a Methodist minister. I also had information from my Mom's side of the family that we had relatives there who also had been in the Confederacy.

I've not-so-jokingly told friends I was the white sheep of my family. Both sides of my extended family had an over-abundance of piety, bigotry, militarism, and an abiding love for the losing side in the War Between the States. I saw my share of Confederate flags growing up. I scandalized my family by rejecting nearly everything they believed in and prayed to. I openly disavowed the Confederacy and told my relatives I would have fought on the Union side, which is true. Not only was slavery an abomination, but for dirt farmers of the South to take up arms against their country to fight at the behest of profiteering plantation owners to me is the height of patriotic misdirection and proof of the effectiveness of propaganda when it is drilled into the masses.

My relatives were not amused.

Not all of them disowned me, however. My cousin Rick Graves, the one who became a Lutheran chaplain and major in the U.S. Army, against the tide of Confederacy sympathies among the Graves family joined the Sons of Union Veterans of the Civil War. He had discovered that some of our direct descendants left the South to join the Union side. Rick and his father, my Uncle Richard, dug deeper into our genealogy than any of my other relatives. As I report elsewhere in this book they discovered our ancestors included a Captain Thomas Graves who was an early settler in the Jamestown, Virginia colony. I suppose that there is some prestige associated with knowing your ancestors were among the first to settle this great land, like those glitterati who claim their forebears came over on the Mayflower, but I can't say that much of that sparkle ever rubbed off on me.

As I stated earlier, Cousin Rick also helped dispel the notion that we, the Graveses, were Scots-Irish. Our genealogy indicates we were solidly British.

And that was that. Until the DNA results arrived.

There are two plans available from 23andMe. One is simply the percentages of your ancestry—where your people are from. The other plan gets into your medical history and whether or not you may be predisposed to certain diseases and so forth. Now I don't know about you, but I would be terrified to learn that I had an 80% chance of getting some dread disease based on me spitting in a tube. I would spend the rest of my life sleeping with one eye open, keeping watch for the grim reaper to come swinging his scythe. No thank you.

So I opened the report online and looked at the long list of ethnic groups and the check marks next to the ones that pertained to me. I assumed everyone in the U.S., no matter their background, would be a Heinz 57 of races. That we all had traces of Asian, Latino, American Indian, South Pacific, Jewish, and African. After all, in the Humanities classes I teach at LeMoyne-Owen College in Memphis there it is right there in the textbook that we all, everyone on Earth, are related to Lucy, otherwise known as AL 288-1, discovered in Ethiopia in 1974. The world's granny.

My DNA analysis showed that 99.6% of me comes from a small part of Western Europe. I am nearly all British with a smattering of Irish and Scottish thrown in. There is about a 15% mixture of German and French, which is common among British-descended people. Shockingly, I have no trace of East European, Hispanic, American Indian, Asian, South Pacific, Jewish, or any other ethnicity. Except way down the list one thing more stood out. I am 0.4% West African.

I knew it. Like Billy Bob Thornton says in that movie *Primary Colors* when he tells the Hotchkiss-educated black guy, "I'm blacker than you are . . . I can feel it." One African wife and one African-American girlfriend used to tell me they thought I had some black in me. We'd laugh about it. And now I know it's true. If I were made up of 200 jigsaw puzzle pieces, 199 would be European, but one stand-out piece would be African. I can hear my Dad and my Granddad

Graves spinning. What would they say had they known this? Would it have in any way altered their racist underpinnings? What would my Granddad's Klansmen brethren have said knowing that at least one drop of Negro was in John Graves' blood? Of course, I'd be willing to bet every single one of those Arkansas Klansmen also had a drop or two or three.

So how do I feel knowing that a small part of Africa is in me? I find it hilarious. I'm wondering how I can bring this up with my students at LeMoyne-Owen College. How will they react if I tell them I'm one two-hundredth African? As one of my friends jokingly put it, "Tom, you still a honky."

Does this explain why I've had this long-time appreciation for the special beauty of black women? Does it explain why I went to Africa and married a Senegalese woman? Does it explain this weird attraction I've had to Africa my whole life and why I want to go back there and continue my travels? Does it explain me writing a biography of bluesman Robert Johnson? Does it explain why I'm reading an epic biography of Ethel Waters as I write this? Does it explain why I'm writing up my application to get a Fulbright teaching grant to teach in Swaziland?

Don't know. But today I have a much sharper image of just who I am. The hundred dollars I paid to spit in that tube? Worth every penny.

And the Colored Girls Go…

I'm thinking it began with Diana Ross and the Supremes. As a white boy growing up in Memphis in the early 1960s, there were no beauty models as such for black women. The society I grew up in taught me that Negroes were an inferior people, an inferior race, and that their perceived ugliness wasn't just about their dusky skin and kinky hair, but their broad noses and big lips as well. Not to mention their big, glistening white teeth and protruding eyeballs when they were frightened. Even the way they walked and talked was eccentric and funny.

As a child I remember my playmates and I kidding around with each other and asking if we would ever kiss a (you know what). Invariably we would feign sickness at the thought and say, "Ugh! Never!" You've got to remember that a version of apartheid was in effect when I was in grade school and very few of us knew blacks on any intimate basis. No one in my Bethel Grove neighborhood, which was solidly blue collar, had black maids or nannies. They simply couldn't afford them. Maids and nannies were for rich people.

Many children when I was coming up repeated the known scientific fact that blacks had purple blood. Several I knew swore they had seen it.

"Why do niggers run so fast?" I remember someone asking. "Because white people chase them all the time."

Here is a typical schoolyard rhyme:

I see your heinie
So black and shiny
It makes me giggle
To see it wiggle

I cannot remember when I first became aware of Lena Horne. I do recall how she was considered a great beauty, perhaps the most beautiful black person in the world. I also remember—and still think—that her features were remark-ably white. (Don't demur. The great critic John Simon said virtually the same thing about Halle Berry, that she looked like a Caucasian with a nice tropical tan.)

I recently watched the film that put Lena Horne on the world stage, *Cabin in the Sky*, where she, the femme fatale in the story, was pitted against the dowdier Ethel Waters. Sitting bejeweled in a black nightclub she indeed radiated great beauty but looked almost nothing like the cast surrounding her, particularly Waters. Miss Waters, who was notoriously protective of her turf and her persona, did everything on the set of *Cabin in the Sky* except stab Horne in the back, literally that is. She worked overtime to undermine the dazzling up-and-comer. Which led to some fantastic fireworks on screen between them. Had the two been the same age—Miss Waters was nearly twice the age of Horne—I have no doubt who would have blown the other right off the camera. Waters in her youth—called Sweet Mama Stringbean when first starting out—not only was one of the best shimmy dancers in Harlem, but had a voice that could make the angels weep. She was slim, curvy, and a stone cold knockout. And ain't nothin' about her that looked white. In her later years when Waters toured with the Billy Graham Crusade a lot of younger people, myself included, had no idea this wonderful grandmother type, beloved by millions, had once upon a time been the hottest thing on long legs. Miss Waters' religiosity was no put on; she had a prayer room in every place she lived. But she lived life explicitly on her own terms. I can't help but wonder if the Billy Graham organization was aware that Miss Waters kept male *and* female lovers her whole life and felt her private affairs were her private affairs. She saw nothing wrong with her sexual appetites and inclinations.

And just for the record, the song Lena Horne is most identified with, "Stormy Weather," was Ethel Waters' hit long before Hollywood let Horne have a go at it.

About the time I learned a thing or two about the birds and the bees, around the age of ten, the refrain had changed from would I kiss a black woman to would I do something a good bit naughtier. The response was still the same. "Ugh!"

Until we all saw Diana Ross and the Supremes on television, that is. The Motown record label did much more than simply make great records. They were a Detroit-based industry that heavily promoted their full product line and that included selling their artists as stars. Motown head Berry Gordy was a black businessman who knew that in order to reach its full potential Motown had to crossover to the far larger, far more lucrative white market. To do that his artists had to appeal to white tastes. To that end Motown artists were carefully groomed, coiffed, and outfitted. They were taught how to speak the Queen's English, which fork to use, and how to stick out one's pinky while sipping a cup of tea. Gordy took a special interest in Diana Ross. There were many who thought the other Supremes, Florence Ballard in particular, were better singers. But it was Ross who had the eye appeal, the one the camera loved.

With their sequined gowns, long eyelashes that seemed to beckon "come hither," slinky stage moves, and breathy vocals, the Supremes broke through the "would you?" barrier.

We would.

We would, we would, we would.

It wasn't long before the world seemed to be full of gorgeous black women. Closer to my age was Millie Small, the Jamaican sensation, who introduced the world to what would evolve into reggae music with her smash hit "My Boy Lollipop." Millie was just a teenager, dressed in the mod fashions of the day, and was a white boy's vision with her delicate curves and ripe Jamaican patois, which was deliciously exotic.

Mattel's Lt. Uhura Barbie doll. Still sexy after all these years.

But none of them had the effect that Nichelle Nichols did on *Star Trek*. Nichols, of course, played Lt. Uhura, bridge officer on the crew of the Starship Enterprise. I was fourteen years old when *Star Trek* first aired and like every teenaged boy in America I never missed an episode. Each show was endlessly discussed with classmates and a lot of the conversation centered around Uhura. I don't think there was a white boy alive at the time who didn't have a crush on Lt. Uhura. Not only was she inarguably beautiful by whatever standard, not only did she have legs up to there barely covered by her mini-skirted uniform, not only did she have a voice that purred, but she was formidably smart too, an indispensable crew member who kept right up with the emotional captain and the imperturbable first officer, Spock. She could be one of the boys but she was most definitely one of the girls.

Then there was the episode where Captain Kirk kisses

Uhura, which was long-believed to be the first interracial kiss on American television until an earlier kiss or two were found in some long-buried archives. The *Star Trek* episode, "Plato's Children," as I recall took place on a planet where aliens entered the minds of the crew of the Enterprise. Thus when the kiss occurred it was not consummated by the free wills of Kirk and Uhura. I suppose that made it all right.

Reportedly, the network braced itself for a deluge of protests and hate mail, which did not materialize. Why? My take on it is that *everyone* wanted to kiss Uhura and felt that Captain Kirk was one lucky sonofabitch. Nichelle Nichols, who was a well-known singer and stage actress prior to *Star Trek*, wanted to leave the show after the first season.

When Dr. Martin Luther King Jr. met Nichols and told her how much he admired her on *Star Trek* she told him her plans for leaving the show. He told her in no uncertain terms that she shouldn't do that. He told her that she may not realize it, but she was a great role model for blacks, particularly black females. She was treated as an equal as a crew member of the Enterprise, integral to the ship's mission to explore "strange new worlds." She wasn't a sex object (even though she was damned sexy). She wasn't servile. She was a professional. Her role as a military officer was never questioned or in doubt.

Like that future spaceman Neil Armstrong would suggest a year later, Lt. Uhura was a small step for racial progress, but a giant leap in terms of racial perceptions.

Big-Legged Woman

AS LONG AS I can remember I have loved girls. Some of my earliest memories are of the electric jolt I got from being around pretty girls, the way they talked, the way they walked, the way they smelled, everything about them. When I was about five years old, the little girl next door taught me to play Tarzan and Jane. We would swing from the trees and do the Tarzan yell and then, at her command, lay it on hot and heavy with the kissing. These were pre-school lessons I would not forget. I had adult relationships where the kissing wasn't half as passionate as those Tarzan and Jane days of my childhood. Karen, the little girl next door, sure knew her business. Not many in my future lived up to the Jane standard.

Around this same time period, friends of the family came to visit. They had a little girl my age. As the adults were talking in the den, the little girl and I went off to play with toys in the living room. While we were playing pretend, this little girl, Robin, without prompting pulled up her skirt and quickly yanked down her panties, giving me a very clear view of a private beach that didn't look a thing like my private beach.

Unsurprisingly I said, "Do that again."

She obliged and this time kept the panties down. Then she began to dance and parade around. I felt as if I'd been plugged into a 220 volt socket. Every synapse in my body was singing hallelujahs. This was such a wonderful happenstance that I decided to pull down my trousers as well and join the parade, or as I called it then, our "Naked Circus." Naked Circus was the most joyful game I had ever played until my Mom swept into the living room, ordered me to pull my pants up, and wore my little behind out. I was sent to bed, but not without Mom telling me what a sinner I was and watching as I had to pray to a merciful God for forgiveness. Even then there was something inside me that rebelled against this kind of prudery. I thought that nothing that made me feel that good could be that bad. I was pretty certain the Devil didn't make me do it.

Integration happened at my school when I was in the fifth grade, which story I have told here. However, it was sixth grade before any sizeable group of blacks was enrolled. I was on the Safety Patrol, and a couple of the black girls broke school rules by running when they weren't supposed to. When I told them not to run, they sassed me, which of course ticked me off and I reported them. I was then told to go and tell their teacher. This teacher made me tell the whole class who the rule-breakers were and to point them out. Every eye was on me. All of a sudden this telling-on-someone thing wasn't such a grand idea. When I pointed out the two girls who had caused offense they gave me stink eyes that stink right now. That was the first and last time I ever reported anyone.

It never would have crossed my mind to think of any of

these black girls in any sexual or romantic sense. They simply weren't on the radar. I can just imagine what might have happened if I had snuck up on one of them and stolen a kiss on the cheek, as I had done many times with my childhood sweetheart, Jessica. I was crossing the street with Jessica on Valentine's Day one year and decided to steal a kiss—aye, I was a bold lad—and when I did I spilled a whole box of valentines on the crosswalk, holding up traffic, and making a lot of parents pretty annoyed. But that kiss was worth it, heh.

When rumors began to circulate that blacks were moving into the Bethel Grove neighborhood, Dad decided to pull up stakes and move to the lily-white Parkway Village subdivision way out in the suburbs, our first ever move as a family. At first there were no blacks in my new schools. Eventually a few blacks who lived within the district were assigned to my middle and high school, Sheffield. In my junior year, a housing project was built on the perimeter of the Sheffield district, and ghetto kids attended the school. It was not an easy or entirely peaceful integration.

I would have recoiled at the idea of romance with any of these blacks. However, there was a notable exception. A black classmate named Debra Harris made an appearance in a school skit that I couldn't quite get out of my mind. Debra was not one of the blacks from the projects. She lived somewhere in the district. Debra was a full-figured girl, attractive if not exactly beautiful, and sported a large afro, which was in vogue at the time. She was what the blues singers would have called "a big-legged woman." She had curves in all the right places and the way she walked she knew it. Debra also was friendly and funny. She was well-liked by pretty much everyone and had no problem flitting from social group to social group depending on her whims. At a class assembly she and another black, a very quiet young man named Jimmy Tate who lived in a deeply wooded area of the district that was without running water, performed a pantomime of the then-popular song "I Gotcha" by Joe Tex. Debra played the girl in question in the song, and repeatedly turned her back on the beseeching male who kept ordering her to "Give it here." Of course the song is loaded with double entendres and exactly what the girl was supposed to give her suitor was not in question. We all knew what he wanted.

Debra in a yearbook photo of the "I Gotcha" skit in her cat suit.

What made the skit unforgettable was that Debra was dressed in a cat suit—black leotards with a cat tail attached, cat ears, whiskers. She knew how to strut her cat stuff. And I knew that if I were stranded in the cloakroom with Debra during a blizzard I would have happily leapt across that racial line, wrath of Dad or no wrath of Dad.

About a year or two later I went to the neighborhood Mc-Donald's to grab some fast food.

I was concentrating on the menu when a familiar voice said, "Well, hello there Tommy Graves."

It was Debra Harris working the counter and she had said that in an unbelievably sexy tone.

"Well, hello yourself, Debra Harris. What are you up to these days?" I hastily replied.

We chatted for another minute, I got my burgers and fries, and left. But I never forgot that encounter and how way, way down deep I would have liked to make a little time with her.

Debra has disappeared into the mist from all media I've tapped into to try and find her. I would assume at some point she married, changed her last name, had children, and moved on with her life. I certainly hope she is not one of my former classmates we would have to put in the "In Memoriam" file, which has occurred more and more frequently as I've aged. Too often my high school reunions have been either all-white or nearly all-white. Years ago I was on a committee planning one of our first reunions. Someone asked if we should invite any of the blacks. After all those years there was still resentment over the Walter Simmons housing project and how those students changed life at Sheffield High School. I began to name off some of the black students I definitely wanted to invite. Debra was one of them. Over the intervening years this kind of stance has softened. Several blacks have attended the reunions and by all appearances had a good time, but the majority has not shown up and many are simply gone without a social media trace. I have put out several feelers for Debra. To no avail.

The Tao of Kim

ONE OF MY BEST friends is about six years older than me
and a veteran of the Vietnam War. How I met Kim Lemser is
over our mutual love for electric blues. The Parkway Village
neighborhood I lived in at the time, when I was nearing my
junior year in high school, was unusually tight and friendly.
Everyone knew everyone and we all socialized. On pleasant
evenings people sat in lawn chairs in their driveways and
visited. My dad worked for the telephone company and got a
discarded telephone pole that he erected off the concrete patio
in our backyard, turning it into a makeshift basketball court.
It was small, but was big enough for us to have rowdy games
virtually the whole year long. Most couples in our neighborhood were much younger than my parents. These young
fathers, in their twenties and early thirties, loved to come over
to our house to shoot basketball with us. In fact, they taught
me how to play the game and taught me well.

Another older couple lived down the street, Dick and
Juanita, who were roughly the same age as my parents, and
we all heard about their son, Kim, who was in Vietnam.
Another friendly neighbor was the first person I knew who

had a genuine real stereo hi-fi. For you gearheads he had a Dynaco tube amplifier, a Bang and Olufsen turntable, and Fisher speakers. I spent virtually every penny I made on record albums. Sometimes before I would even open the album cover, I would take it to this neighbor's house and ask if I could play it on his hi-fi. This is how I first heard the *Sgt. Pepper* album by the Beatles. To this day I don't think I've ever had a more powerful listening experience.

This neighbor bought one of the first cassette decks ever marketed. I knew about reel-to-reel tape recorders, but as fine as the sound was, they were impractical in everyday use. Cassettes were the new thing and catching on big. Vinyl records were not popular in the hot and humid climate of Vietnam, where they could easily warp in the heat and the heavy dust ruined both records and the gear. American soldiers quickly adapted to cassettes.

Everyone on Navaho, my street, knew I was fanatical about rock music and had a lot of albums. They thought perhaps my tastes would coincide with Kim Lemser's over in Vietnam. Kim had even asked his parents specifically to get him Mountain's *Climbing* album on cassette. Well, I had that record in my collection and my neighbor with the hi-fi could record it to cassette tape. They asked me if I might recommend some similar albums, and I did. They recorded those too and sent them off to Kim Lemser, A.P.O., Vietnam.

I thought nothing more about it until I heard Kim, whom I had never met, would be coming home on leave. A few days later there was a knock at our back door, and a slender, nice-looking older guy was standing there who I couldn't place. He introduced himself as Kim Lemser, the guy in the Army, and he asked if he might go through my record collection and pick a few other albums to record to cassette that he could take back with him to 'Nam. It seems that my other choices that were sent to him hit on all cylinders. When I showed him the electric guitar, my first, I had just gotten, a 1959 Gibson Melody Maker, he was even more interested. He had been in a garage band himself and loved electric guitars, biding his time to get another one until he was out of the service. We talked a long time about a lot of things.

I, in turn, paid Kim visits at his parents' house down the street. He invited me to go riding around with him as he re-immersed himself in Memphis while on leave, going back to his old haunts in his Berclair neighborhood and slowly reconnecting with old friends. Kim was not in combat in Vietnam; he was a radio operator who was almost always on the periphery of the action but not actually in it. That didn't stop the occasional incoming fire, and he told me about explosions outside his radio truck that had him diving for cover. He also told me about the fear of driving down jungle roads that might be booby-trapped or receive sniper fire. This was heady stuff to a 15-year-old.

There were other things he taught me. About the party girls in Vietnam who would pleasure the G.I.s. Although I was loathe to admit it to most of the guys I palled around with, like them, I was a virgin. All we talked about was girls and sex. It was tattooed in our heads. But talk—*big* talk at that—is all it was. Bullshit was the order of the day. To have a friend who had not only done it, but done it many times, many ways, with all different kinds of girls, was like getting a master class in sex. I asked a million questions. I wanted to know everything.

And I wanted to know about drugs. Strike that. I was only really interested in trying marijuana. By this time I was a subscriber to *Rolling Stone* magazine. Pot smoke practically wafted off the pages when you opened that month's edition. With the stark exception of Frank Zappa who pointedly did not use drugs, everyone else was doping like madmen. By this time Jimi Hendrix, Janis Joplin, Jim Morrison, and others had met their ends from drug use. Drugs were everywhere. Except in Sheffield school. Drugs hadn't made a significant appearance there just yet.

I was scared of heavy drugs, particularly hallucinogenic drugs like LSD. But I was pretty sure marijuana was relatively harmless and that I wouldn't die from smoking a few joints. Vietnam, of course, was a pharmacopeia of recreational drugs for G.I.s. My new friend was well-acquainted with just about all of them and was able to tell me in great detail exactly what they were all about. We scored some hashish—which I naively thought was the same thing as regular pot—on the Highland Strip, the hippie Mecca of the day in Memphis. I knew a guy there and he helped us score. I had never had more than a taste of liquor in my life. I had never experienced a high of any kind. I expected the high from this marijuana thing to be nothing more than a mild euphoria.

As anyone with experience can tell you, hashish is potent, powerful stuff. It hit me like The Cannonball Express. Everything felt . . . *different*. Everything looked . . . *different*.

We bought orange sodas and when the first sip hit the back of my throat it was as if I had developed some supersense of taste. Nothing before or since has ever tasted so *orange*. When I got home I immediately went to bed, but not without an inquisition from my Mom about where I had been. I could barely get the words out. The next morning I still felt slightly high and was worried I'd never feel normal again. I prayed to God to spare me from this awful thing. The day after that I felt fine, normal. And I was ready to try pot again.

That was my drug year. Drugs invaded my school to the point they were practically falling out of the lockers. There were the jocks, the freaks, and the nerds. I was considered a freak, but I never grew my hair very long, and never got that far out with my clothes. I didn't try any other drugs, even though they were offered to me almost on a daily basis. I smoked a good bit of marijuana that year, got to know it pretty well. One thing that no one had told me about is these awful thoughts that would run through my head while under the influence. I would become terrified that the police would find a grain or two of marijuana and hustle me off to a dungeon where I would spend the rest of my life beating rats off my decomposing body. Death would permeate my thoughts. Paranoia they would call it, and the more I smoked the more unpleasant it got.

I was rousted from a school assembly that year along with a couple of other freaks because I was suspected of harboring drugs. I had none, so they didn't find anything. But with the entire school body witnessing me being hustled out of the auditorium, you can imagine the rumors that flew. I didn't like it one bit that I was labeled a doper. I've explained that my parents were devout Southern Baptists who never missed a Sunday morning or Sunday night. My brother and I were required to go. I remember the Sunday School superintendent telling me that her children—who were in grade school at an entirely different school—had told her that they had heard that I was busted for selling LSD. This was a miserable time for me. By senior year I had completely given up smoking pot and never really fooled with any other drugs later except a sniff or two, a puff or two, for social purposes, later. And that was mostly to appease girls I was with so as not to appear to be a stick in the mud. But I didn't like it.

Fast forward a couple of years. I had turned 18 which meant I could get a real job other than throwing newspapers. I was preparing for fall admission to Memphis State University and did not yet know what my course of study would be. My friend Kim Lemser had finished his tour of duty in 'Nam and was back home in Memphis. His father was in the auto parts business and had gotten him a job at Parts Distributors Warehouse, or PDW for short. Kim got one of the better warehouse jobs at PDW, working the will call desk, filling orders for people who came in off the street for auto parts. Kim's dad also got me a job at PDW, loading trucks. It was a hard, dirty, labor-intensive job that paid minimum wage. But it put gas in my 1965 Mustang, which my Dad had bought me upon graduation from high school. Finally I could take girls out in my own car.

A lot of very tough black guys, many of them my age,

worked at PDW. I got along well with most of them and those I didn't get along with were too scared to mess with me because I was under the protection of a sweetheart of a black guy I will call Andrew. Andrew took an instant liking to me; he had a literary bent and would write verse on cardboard that he would hang up around his work station. He boxed up parts and sometimes I helped him. He had been a ranked football player in high school and was built like a Caterpillar tractor. He had huge biceps, a neck like a Spanish bull, and could flip a switch that made him look like the most ferocious badass in town. He struck fear in the hearts of the homeboys who liked to stir up shit. But to me he was Gentle Ben.

There was a little office off the main warehouse where a small group of graphic artists worked on catalogs for the company. Occasionally the artists would need to walk through the warehouse to go to the catalog room, where clerks took phone orders. No one paid them any attention unless *she* walked through the warehouse. She was a petite, gorgeous little black girl, in her early twenties, who was always made up, always superbly-dressed, and in her tight mini-skirts would bring all activity in the warehouse to a dead halt when she walked through. I'm not joking when I say everything would stop—it was like something out of a Marx Brothers movie.

I remember a black guy turning to me as she walked by one day and saying, "Man, I'd turn her upside down and lick her like a lollipop."

At this time Kim and I had gone our separate paths and although we were still on speaking terms, rarely did. Once he had gotten settled back in Memphis he, quite naturally, sought out friends his own age and left the kid, me, to his own devices. We both still loved electric guitars and when we did spare a minute to chat it was generally guitar talk.

I worked at PDW for a year, hating it, and then got what to a student was a dream job, working as a clerk for what was then called First National Bank of Memphis. It was still a minimum wage job but I was working with a much better class of riff-raff.

Sometime around my sophomore year of college I heard that my old acquaintance Kim Lemser was involved in an accident. Everyone in the neighborhood was talking about it. He had taken a girl—a *black* girl—to a movie drive-in. When his car wouldn't start he poured some gasoline in the carburetor to see if that might spark it and get it to turn over. He told the girl to wait for his signal before she turned on the ignition. She misunderstood and turned on the ignition switch as he was pouring the gas, which caused it to explode in Kim's face. He had to be rushed to the hospital with severe facial burns. But what everyone was talking about was Kim taking a black girl—!!—to the drive-in, obviously for immoral purposes.

Kim was an only child and his parents doted on him. When they came to see him in the hospital he wasn't keen on them being there. He didn't want to discuss it. When it was determined that no major damage had been done and that in time he would fully recover, they wanted to inquire about this black woman he was with. One effect Vietnam had on a lot of veterans was a complete disregard for being preached to or told what to do. Kim wasn't having any of it.

About a decade after this accident, Kim and I caught back

up with one another and have been close friends ever since. We touch base just about every day. We joke about it saying we stay in touch just to make sure we're both still alive. A few years back he was in a mood to talk about his accident at the drive-in.

He said, "You knew who I was with that night didn't you?"

I replied that I didn't. I had just assumed it was some pick-up girl he had met at a club or bar somewhere in town and had taken to the drive-in for some backseat thrills.

"That was Dell I was with," he said.

I didn't know who he was talking about.

"Do you remember that cute black girl who worked at PDW in the Advertising Department who'd walk through the warehouse…"

"Oh God, THAT WAS YOUR GIRLFRIEND???!!!"

And so it was. Some guys have all the luck.

When I started having some of my own black girlfriends Kim said, "Man, you got that from me."

Do Black Folks Like Elvis?

MANY TIMES IN MY high school years Kim Lemser and I sat intently listening to blues albums on his portable stereo, discussing blues licks and trying to duplicate them on our guitars. Kim introduced me to the slide guitar of Elmore James and the biting snarl of Albert King's lead guitar recorded across town at Stax Records. I introduced him to my favorite blues guitarist, Peter Green of Fleetwood Mac, and the early LPs by John Mayall's Bluesbreakers that featured virtuoso work by Eric Clapton, Peter Green, and Mick Taylor.

Just a few years earlier I spent all my newspaper route money on rock albums and every month read *Hit Parader* magazine, the only magazine devoted to rock music available in my neighborhood. I found my first issue of *Rolling Stone* magazine in Pine Bluff, Arkansas and sent off for a subscription. I kept reading about this new type of music called "blues." In the pages of these magazines were afro-haired white boys playing shit-cool electric guitars in thundering bands such as Cream, Fleetwood Mac, The Butterfield Blues Band, Canned Heat, and many, many others. In interviews with these guitar gods they kept mentioning guys like B.B. King, Albert King, and others. Why, I could have sworn that those were black guys who played in the Memphis clubs. I had seen those colorful posters on light poles all over Orange Mound advertising those same names in big letters. It was through those bell-bottomed English lads that I discovered the blues in my own backyard. By the time I got my first driver's license, I had a vintage Gibson Melody Maker guitar and was learning blues as fast as I could.

With my beloved Gibson Melody Maker guitar circa 1971.

Kim and I both had learned to switch radio channels often, checking out what was happening on WDIA-AM in Memphis for example, the self-described "black spot on your radio dial." The airwaves at that time were largely segregated: whites listened to white stations and blacks listened to black stations. But Elvis and rock and roll changed all that up. Blacks in Memphis clearly loved Elvis Presley and his music, and whites in Memphis, unlike in many parts of the U.S., were buying the original recordings of Little Richard and Chuck Berry rather than the tepid remakes by the likes of Pat Boone. Kim and I also discovered the lively and often hilarious commercials on WDIA as announced by hometown favorites such as the great Rufus Thomas, who in later years told me my favorite Elvis story.

Few Memphians have been so beloved by this city as Rufus Thomas, who will forever be considered the master of ceremonies for Memphis. Rufus had the first hit record for both Sun Records and later for Stax Records. Songs of his like "Walkin' the Dog" are staples of rock and roll and his dance craze the Funky Chicken and its companion novelty song made him a household name in the '60s, when he was dubbed "The World's Oldest Teenager." During all this time Thomas never gave up his seat at the microphone for radio station WDIA which was beamed into thousands of black households every weekday, where he was considered a member of the family. He was recognized everywhere he went in Memphis, by blacks and whites, and loved the attention. When he was up in age and getting around with the help of a walker, he had a raccoon tail attached to the cross handle, ever the cool cat.

In 1994 I approached Thomas about the two of us working together on his autobiography. No one, and I mean *no one*, had better stories than Rufus Thomas. I knew that an autobiography from Rufus would be a major addition to the music book canon. I conducted a lengthy interview with Rufus and prepared a tight proposal for prospective publishers. We instantly secured a prominent literary agent who specialized in music books, but much to my disappointment she could not rouse much interest in the big New York publishers who simply were not that aware of Rufus or his stature here in Memphis.

I always loved his story about trying to play Elvis on the black station WDIA when Elvis came out with his first Sun records. Here is the story as told to me by Rufus:

Let me give you a picture of how things were with Elvis back in those days. They say that Elvis used to go up and down Beale Street, to the clubs and things, but I never saw Elvis in a club. Never once saw him on Beale Street. Now, I'm not saying he *wasn't* there, I'm just saying I never *saw* him there.

I was the only black jock who was playing Elvis's music on the radio when he came out, on WDIA (the nation's first radio station with all-black programming—*ed.*). David James, the program director for WDIA who was also in charge of operations and who was white, thought that he could think for black folks. Ain't no one person who can think for no one group. It just doesn't work.

I was playing Elvis on my radio show and he stopped me. He said, "Black folks don't like Elvis."

He ran operations for the station, so what was I gonna do? I wanted to keep my job, so I didn't play Elvis anymore.

Well, WDIA used to have the Starlight Review and the Goodwill Review every year for handicapped black children, because they didn't have any way of getting to school, no way of even trying to get an education. If you were handicapped you were just *there*. We put these shows on in order to raise funds to provide for these kids. We got schools, a bus, teachers, principals, the whole works—that's what this money was for.

George Klein (a white deejay for radio station WHBQ and a close friend of Elvis—ed.) brought Elvis backstage at one of our Goodwill Reviews at Ellis Auditorium. My youngest daughter was three years old at the time. When Elvis was backstage my little daughter was pulling on him and said, "You my boyfriend." He sat down with her and talked to her. I have a picture of her there with Elvis, sitting on his knee.

I played the part of an Indian on that program. Everything is going, the show was going good. One of the fellows who was in charge of the program, sort of the stage manager, wanted to show Elvis on stage close to the beginning of the show. I told him, his name was Don Kinds, I said, "Don, don't do that. If you put Elvis up there in the front of that show the show is over. *Don't do that.*" I guess he was thinking—he had that same mentality as David James—that black folks would just see Elvis and that would be it. No big deal. But I told him, *"Do not do that!* Put him at the *end* of the show."

I took Elvis by his hand—I've got a picture of that one too—and led him on stage. And when I got him on stage he did him one of them kind of things [gives his leg a shake] for just about a minute, made that little appearance there. And that show was OVER! Those people clamored and went on trying to get to that man!

And the next day I went back to playing Elvis.

Top Cat

I STARTED DATING MY first real girlfriend the night I graduated from high school. We dated hot and heavy that whole summer and when I started my freshman year in college and she began her senior year of high school, the social forces at play inevitably pulled us apart. A pattern seemed to set in the college years to come where I would have a steady girlfriend starting in the spring, lasting through summer, and edging into fall when we would break up. Then there would be fitful, intermittent, non-productive dating— catch as catch can—until a steady girl would emerge the next spring, like daffodils.

Another disturbing problem developed as I began the game of dating roulette. The more desirable the intended date, the more frozen and tongue-tied I would become. As loquacious as I was under normal conditions, I had to fight for conversation when a real good-looker was sitting next to me. Making even the mildest of moves was fraught with uncertainty and klutziness. "Whoops, sorry," was an all-too-common utterance as I spilled a drink, fumbled a kiss, didn't know what to say when I escorted a girl to her front door.

In short, I was a nervous wreck. A universal characteristic of women is that they don't like timid, stuttering, cowering men. They like confidence. Of which my tank was running low.

I'm not sure how I did it, but my attempts to woo and charm were surprisingly successful on occasion with girls who were way out of my league. I often set my sights too high and didn't know what to do once I had gotten these beautiful creatures into my Ford Mustang. It usually didn't take but a date or two for things to slide into the relationship abyss.

Going completely against the grain of the Don Knotts inside me was how smooth I was around the foxy black girls I worked with at First National Bank, a part-time job while I attended college. I was hired initially for a summer job where we filled out forms consolidating information for computer entry. It was simple, brain-free work. The bank had hired about 20 students from a cross-section of Memphis-area colleges. Nearly every one of them, unlike me, was a brilliant scholarship student. A number of my fellow employees were female black students, many of whom had scholarships from the prestigious and upper-crusty Southwestern, now named Rhodes College. I can say with assurance that they were all smarter than me.

Having spent a year working at Parts Distributors Warehouse among a large group of working class black males, I had learned the art of shucking and jiving and could keep right up with them. I applied this skill set to the black girls I worked with at First National Bank and they got quite a kick out of this cocky white boy who was always up to jokes and mischief. I flirted outrageously with them, all in fun, not a thought or a shred of real romantic interest. There wasn't a thing about me they wouldn't rag on: "You sure do like that cologne you wearing. I bet that's some of that high-dollar Aqua Velva from your daddy." "Them bell bottoms dragging the floor. You gonna make them ragged." "You just wake up? Your hair looks like a rooster."

They crowned me with the sobriquet Top Cat, after the smarmy, self-assured cartoon character. In the bullpen where we all worked, the volume level of our raucous discussions would get so high we would receive complaints from the surrounding departments. We were often told to "keep it down."

When the summer was over most of the students left and returned back to school. A handful of us were retained for part-time work and merged with another department, a department comprised entirely of females. Not a bad way to go for a college boy.

By this time I knew people all over the bank building. We held long breaks in the cafeteria where the young people, mostly college students like me, would get together and socialize. One of my new colleagues was a very attractive brunette named Cecelia who was about five years older than me and married. I got the impression from her no-nonsense demeanor and aloof airs that she was a real bitch-on-wheels, someone to definitely avoid tangling with.

As I would talk and carry-on and cut-up, particularly with the black girls, I noticed that Cecelia was listening in and I could occasionally spot the beginnings of a smile as I cracked a joke. About this time I got my first job as a writer: I became the film critic for the college newspaper *The Helmsman*. I was only a sophomore, but I convinced the editors that I could do the job and write well enough for publication. I don't get the feeling as a college professor today that students take these kinds of positions, which of course are unpaid, very seriously. But let me assure you the staff of *The Helmsman* took their jobs seriously indeed as did the faculty of the Journalism Department, where by the way I had decided I found my major. I didn't just go to the movies and write a few blurbs about them. I had already studied the great film critics of the day and knew the world of cinema backwards and forwards. Every spare minute of my time was spent reading John Simon, Pauline Kael, Andrew Sarris, Rex Reed, and numerous others. I spent hours and hours in the school library. I soaked them all in, a film critic sponge. (Interestingly, today I am in touch with Simon and Reed through my indie publishing company, The Devault-Graves Agency. I still have my heroes. Pauline Kael, on the other hand, I have not so fond memories of. A story for another day.)

I would bring new issues of *The Helmsman* to work with me and regale everyone with my perceptions on the latest films. I held forth, as they say, probably to the irritation of many of my co-workers and visibly so with my supervisor. Cecelia, however, began to take an interest in my film reviews and would chat with me at length about them. This cold fish seemed to be thawing.

Around this time a very cute, petite, perky black girl with a halo of afro on her head named Janet was hired. I could tell she wasn't from Memphis because she didn't have that quick snap!-and-sass common to Memphis black girls. She had a slower, cotton-candy-in-your-mouth accent, from somewhere deep down in the thick of the Mississippi Delta. Her talk may have been slow, but her mind and tongue were lightning quick. She *always* had a funny barb or two in reserve for me. Our back and forth had all the girls up on the 5th floor laughing.

Don't think I wasn't noticing how attractive and sexy these young black women were. I was caught "checking" them on more than one occasion when my eyeballs got a little reckless. Janet told me in front of all the other girls one day that she wanted me to take her to the Mid-South Fair, a big annual event in Memphis. I knew she wasn't serious and I played along. Everyone was amused. But she kept it up. Day after day, week after week she'd be asking about going to the fair. She was putting pressure on me in front of the girls to see how I would handle it.

The truth is, play or no play, I would have *loved* to take her to the fair. In fact I daydreamed about it. I knew she would be great fun to take on a date and my fantasies kicked into overdrive thinking what might happen should we be alone together. However, I was living at home all this time I was attending college. I had no place to take a girl for any kind of real intimacy. Plus, I didn't want to think what might happen if my Dad found out I had gone out in public with a black girl. Janet's daily importuning about the fair kept me on my toes, thinking of ways to deflect the whole thing while both saving face and making everyone laugh. The fair finally came and went and I was greatly relieved when the matter dropped. Even now I sometimes think back on Janet and wonder what would have happened if I had shown up at her place and opened my car door.

A month or two later I noticed that tiny little Janet seemed to be putting on some weight. Another few weeks went by of no consequence when I noticed a definite bulge in her middle that could only mean one thing—a baby was on its way. Over the next several months our flirting all but stopped. Very little was said about her pregnancy. She had the baby and shortly thereafter came back to work, nothing more to it. She wasn't married and I'm not sure she even had a steady boyfriend. In the world I had been raised in this was something shameful. Out of wedlock. An unmarried woman. A bastard child. All scarlet phrases in the white people world of that time.

I've always believed devoutly in family. The most important role in life in my opinion is to be a good parent, and bringing up a child in a loving family environment is paramount. Family planning is a must. I have always thought that with sexual freedom—which I also believe in—comes a very heavy responsibility. In the back of my mind I couldn't quite forgive Janet for failing her sexual responsibilities. But I must admit one of the factors in these feelings is that this proved that little doll Janet was driving in a convertible down the sexual highway. And I wasn't. I was still, most unhappily, a virgin.

Parking was always a problem at the bank building. There were pricey parking lots nearby, but especially when working part-time and going to college this was prohibitively expensive. So, many of us scoured the side streets hoping to find an available space on the street. This usually entailed a walk of a few blocks to the bank building which in rain and snow was not fun. One spring day I had parked my car on the street and was mindlessly walking the few blocks to work. Around the corner walking on the same sidewalk coming towards me was a trio of blacks, two males, one female, who did not look like the typical residents of the area. They were a bit older than me, by all appearances in their mid-twenties. All three sported hedgerows of afros and the type of clothing, such as black leather, that made me identify them with radical groups such as The Black Panthers. In my memory the males wore sunglasses.

I am ordinarily an amiable enough fellow. When passing people on the street I generally nod and say hello. That's just my Southern manners. As the trio approached I presented a soft smile and noticed three sets of eyes boring into me, scowls clouding their faces. I moved to my far right to allow them to pass me on the sidewalk. In a lightning second I knew that if I didn't step off the sidewalk into the street I was going to be physically forced off the sidewalk. At the last instant, I stepped off the curb and the three hustled straight past me. Had I not moved I either would have been pushed out of the way or perhaps beaten. I could not believe what had just happened. I stopped and looked behind me. They had stopped as well, all three glaring at me with a "whatchu gonna do about it muthafucka?" stance in their body language.

We stared at each other for a few seconds, my jaw hanging open, and then we slowly went our separate ways. That is the only time in my life something like that has happened to me. It is a circumstance not easily forgotten. Still in a semi state of shock, I told everyone at the bank including the black girls I worked with. They all expressed concern and puzzlement. I've often wondered who those people were and why they felt the need to force me off the sidewalk. I'm sure similar scenarios have played out for decades between the races. That thought, however, does not console me.

The ice queen, Cecelia, had by this time become one of my dearest friends and confidants at the bank. She arranged it so that I could spend part of my workday working with her on her specific tasks. I decided one summer that instead of taking summer classes I would work full time at the bank, the long hours which I would soon regret. However, because Cecelia lived close by in my Parkway Village neighborhood, that summer I began to give her a ride in the morning to work. She caught a ride in the evening with another co-worker. Cecelia and I could talk, and did, for hours. We never ran out of topics and gossip to discuss. I had developed quite a crush on this exquisite specimen, because she was all-woman, mature, cultured (she had been to "charm school" in her youth), shapely, and of an elegant beauty that totally captured me. I loved the way she would glide into a room and every eye would be on her. But because she was married I never thought I remotely had a chance with her and so dismissed those thoughts entirely. She was simply a friend, an older, married friend, and I was well-contented with that.

Others, however, suspected something deeper was afoot. I saw a lot of older men at the bank, most of them married, find a way to maneuver into our 5th floor department for the express purpose of chatting up Cecelia. When it came to this kind of obvious flirtation, she had alcohol in her veins. She could blow off someone with a mere glance. The fact she was so warm around me was not lost on anyone. I was oblivious, caught up in my own world. I couldn't see or quite believe that the most desirable woman at First National Bank Operations Center was romantically interested in me.

I finally realized our relationship was more than just friends when some of the girls in the department told me how Cecelia had gone off on some of our co-workers when they were gossiping about me. I let it slip that I was kind of semi-attracted to one of the (white) girls in our department and it created a buzz that got back to both the girl in question and Cecelia. This girl, it turned out, wasn't particularly fond of me and knew some of my high school classmates who weren't particularly fond of me either. When the put-downs started in their little sewing circle Cecelia blew up at them and let them know none of them were deserving of a fine man such as myself. I do have my champions. And detractors.

Cecelia, who didn't especially like to have her picture taken, at First National Bank

Her vehemence during this occurrence is what made several of the girls tell me, "Cecelia may be married, but she likes you Tom." By "likes" they obviously meant "loves."

I was getting burned out at the bank. I enjoyed the people I worked with but the clerical work was drudgery and I was exhausted by the drive downtown and the endless parking problems. I wanted blue skies, a change of pace, something different. When I told Cecelia I was going to quit, she rolled her eyes at me, and for the next few weeks barely spoke to me. She was angry. Really, really angry.

On my very last day somehow it was arranged that I would give her a ride home. That's when it all came out.

"How can you leave me alone with all those people?" she demanded to know. "Damn you Tom Graves."

By the time I pulled up to her house we had sworn solemn oaths to keep in touch—she wouldn't give anyone her phone number, although she had mine—and she reached over and gave me a quick kiss on the cheek, the first time anything physical had transpired between us. It felt like I'd been kissed by a cattle prod, so electrifying was the effect.

Over the next few years I saw Cecelia only a few times. I had gone back to the bank building to visit her and some other friends. Some major changes had come my way in those next couple of years. I had matured myself, and was running with an elite group of hipsters from the Poplar Tunes record store scene. Not to mention my writing world was greatly expanding. As a journalism student I had published substantive articles in some magazines. I was a student god striding around the Journalism building. No other student had ever published long-form journalism—real writing—in serious publications before. That was something you did after graduation.

I was never much of a party boy or a bar hound, but I loved the parties thrown by the Poplar Tunes gang. One night I was in my room sprucing up for a Poplar Tunes party when the family phone rang. It was for me. I recognized the voice immediately: Cecelia.

"My husband is out of town and I was listening to some music and thought you might want to come over and listen to some albums."

I did.

The Dark End of the Street

NOT LONG BEFORE I found myself alone with Cecelia on a Friday night when her husband was out of town, I was 20 years old, nearing my junior year in college and still had not had sex with a woman. I felt a deep, hot shame inside and was psychologically wounded enough to think I was a failure in life, unable to attract a woman who would of her own volition give me her most precious offering. I was confused too. I was popular enough with my fellow Journalism students. I had cachet because I was the film critic for *The Helmsman* and promoted myself around campus as "the writer." And I seemed to be able to get dates with some drop-dead gorgeous young women. But there seemed to be a Berlin Wall between me and sex.

I was determined not to go into my 21st year a virgin. By God something had to be done. Since I had no girlfriend or steady date at that moment, there could be only one other course of action. I would pay for it. I did not have enough money to pay for some high-priced call girl plus I had no idea where to begin to find such a person. At that time there were no real strip clubs in Memphis and I'd never delved into the dark side of Memphis' nascent and scary porno world. I was a naif, a know-nothing, a virgin for God's sake.

But I knew about Vance and Fourth Street. Everybody did. That's where you went for a black street walker, the lowest sexual life form on this green Earth. It was known to be dangerous to fool around in that part of town. Especially if you were white.

You might get robbed. You could wind up stabbed or shot. You might get a beat down just for the fun of it from some gold-toothed gun-toting pimp. And you might get arrested, your name on a rap sheet, a year in the doghouse with your folks, a pariah on campus.

And I was willing to risk all that for one moment of pleasure that I couldn't tell a soul about. But I could say to myself that I was no longer a virgin. That I had crossed the line into the world of sex. I was—finally—a man. Not no boychild. A *man*. I spell M-A-N.

You get the picture.

Friday night, I put fifteen dollars in my wallet. Another twenty in my sock, just in case. I started roaming the down-town area, looking for the exact right spot on Vance and Fourth and for possible places to get the groove on should I find a willing prostitute. It wasn't long before I spotted a clot of high-heeled women strutting at that intersection, just as advertised. On my first pass they waved at me, and I began to shake. I must have driven in a circle around those blocks for half an hour before finally pulling over to draw their attention. Four or five fancy-dressed dark-skinned women without any hesitation crowded up around the passenger side window.

"What you lookin' for, baby?" one of them asked.

"You want a date?" another one inquired.

"Just lookin' for a little bit of a good time," I replied.

Let me describe this scene for you. It was dark on this corner. Pitch dark. These girls came out of the shadows in their shabby but provocative clothing looking like something dredged up out of a *The Walking Dead* episode. At the time, decades before *The Walking Dead*, it all reminded me of scenes of blood-sucking ghouls in those old EC horror comic books. Where the eye sockets were hollow and the mouths gaping and dripping with viscous drool. My instinct was to push the accelerator to the floorboard and head for the covers of my bed. But my loins were on auto pilot.

Out of this bedraggled roost I was forced to choose one. I don't think I've seen a less desirable group of women in my life. Donald Trump would have to sell off his New York penthouse to pay for the dental work these girls needed. I picked the one with the fewest rotten teeth.

It was very apparent that she was as scared of me as I was of her. She asked me repeatedly if I was a cop, which struck me as strange because I didn't think I looked a thing like a cop. We quickly got down to business.

"I can give you a blow for ten dollars," she said as if she were selling socks at a flea market.

I pulled out my wallet, gave her the ten dollars and she could see the extra five dollar bill I had left even though she didn't know about that extra twenty I had hidden in my sock.

"I'll catch the cum for that other five," she added.

I had no idea precisely what she meant, but I thought I'd

better pay it anyway. The money part being transacted, she directed me to a nearby empty parking lot.

It is a good thing I was 20 years old because if I were to repeat such an episode today I would in no way be able to sustain my ardor while in such a state of fear. What man in his sixties wouldn't give up his Social Security for the tumescent strength of his youth? All of me was shaking except the one body part in the spotlight. That night I was made of tungsten steel despite my utter lack of attraction to my car mate.

With one hand she held my right hand down very tightly in a kind of grip. She did this to prevent me from hitting her. I picked up on the fact she must have been hit by johns many times in her line of work. Every time she looked at me I could see fear in her eyes.

With her free hand she unzipped my pants and took my ironwork of a penis into her mouth and made a variety of professional noises and movements that felt like heaven itself.

She kept on and kept on and finally said, "Shit, when you gone cum?"

"I don't know," I answered truthfully.

"Well, maybe we should fuck instead."

I agreed and why not? She peeled off her panties from under the mini-skirt she wore and even in the darkness of my Ford Mustang I could clearly see the Holy Font cloaked in a Holy Forest. In that confined space, lanky me tried my best to contort myself into a position to enter her but as I had no idea what I was doing my penis kept falling out, ker-flump.

"Is it in?"

"Yeah, it in. No wait; now it ain't."

This went on for several minutes until we both gave up—I still don't see how anyone over five foot tall can have sex in a car—and she decided to proceed with fellatio. She was no artist. I know some men reach nirvana in minutes, some in only seconds. Fear is what held back my floodgates but the pure pleasure of the moment finally broke down the defenses.

"It's happening, it's happening, I'm about to………"

And with that John Phillips Sousa tapped his baton and "Stars and Stripes Forever" began to play in the background while comets and fireworks sprayed across the sky. Soldiers saluted as they marched by in parade step.

My nightwatch paramour found an old rag I used to check my oil with and spat a voluminous issue of male love into it, wiped her mouth with the back of her hand, and said "okay." While I hadn't expected any exhortations of passion and tenderness a simple "okay" wasn't exactly the most heart-warming of endearments. She walked in her high heels back to her perch and I would never lay eyes on her again. Unlike my later sex partners, she would never appear in my fantasies or in my dreams.

Immediately afterwards I felt such revulsion and self-loathing that I came very close to vomiting. I didn't feel safe again until I crossed the border back into my white suburbs. I vowed never to do such a disgusting turn again, and I've kept to that promise. Mostly. After a few days I burned the rag still in my car and eventually got past the yuck factor and felt I had actually accomplished something, met a goal in life. However, I did wish my first sexual experience had been with a girl I cared for. I wanted something more beautiful—a choir singing in the background perhaps—and my trip to Vance and Fourth was anything but beautiful. I never really thought about the fact that my first time was with a black woman. The fact she was a nasty-ass downtown street ho is what rubbed me wrong. The fact she was black didn't enter into the equation.

In the aftermath of that night I worried for several weeks that I may have caught a sexual disease. I kept a close watch below the belt for any sign of something wayward down there. But everything stayed pink and rosy and blotch free and functioned as it was supposed to. The only thing that lingered was the memory and godawfulness of the whole thing.

Until I wrote what you've just read, I never told a soul about this first time encounter. I always avoided any discussion that would veer in the direction of "what was your first time like?" and lied to anyone who tried to pin me down on it. Although I was glad I could tell someone truthfully that I was not, technically speaking, a virgin, I was still humiliated by the experience. Having to buy it, once again, made me feel like a failure, a loser.

I stayed far away from that downtown area the rest of my life. There have been a few approaches during foreign travel and some very direct ones in Memphis that I did not turn away during my prowling years. I regret none of it, but I never really went for the "pay me" girls like a lot of guys I knew did. I particularly disliked strip clubs and the naked pests who greet you and cling to you parasitically at such places. I do, however, have some pretty funny stories to tell about some of the less glitzy black strip clubs I visited just to see if the rumors were true about what went on there. They were true.

I wanted to be loved. I wanted to be desired. I never wanted to have to beg a woman for sex or chip away at her resolve in a relationship.

And that's the way I felt until not long after that horror show night at Vance and Fourth when Cecelia, a woman I would never stop loving, called me on the telephone and I knocked on her door on a frigid Friday night where it was warm, very warm, and oh-so-inviting inside.

Crossing the Bridge

MANY TIMES I'VE BEEN asked by white friends how and why I began to date black women. The truth is that after 23 years of marriage to my first wife Katrina I wanted to make up for what I considered lost time, and I wasn't going to abide by anyone's rules other than my own. Everything and anyone was on the table, and my undergraduate years of shyness and hiding behind a façade of one sort or another were over. This was the new Tom.

Another little truth is that black women seemed to find me more attractive and interesting than comparable white women. I always felt that too many white women nurtured fantasies of the "perfect man," the knight in shining armor on his white steed (always with the horses, these white women) who would rescue them from the drudgery of traditional marriage. Of course men nurture their share of fantasies too, clicking their nights away gaping at sex goddesses on the infinite highway of internet porn.

In my senior year of college I had foolishly pursued a coquettish fellow Journalism major who seemed to enjoy nothing more than basking in the attention of a male entourage, of which I merrily belonged. There was endless partying, drinking, dancing, and the occasional illicit substance to take the edge off things. But no intimacies. I kept thinking my ardor would be rewarded at any time, if only I were patient enough, and so I kept tagging along. We went to a concert together and halfway into the performance my "date" deserted me with no explanation. My feelings were quite bruised over this and when I complained later about how I was treated I was met with a shocking outburst of insult and temper that ended that platonic relationship then and there. This girl had a roommate named Katrina Angeletti with whom I had become friendly, a young woman who had impressed me with her Mediterranean beauty, calm demeanor, and sensible outlook, someone the complete opposite of her mercurial and atten-tion-seeking roomie. On a whim I called and asked if she would like to see a film with me. She did and this led to 23 years of weekly cinema trips, if not more. We both loved films and never tired of watching and debating them. Even today when we talk every few months or so we ask what good films the other has seen.

After we began to date I would occasionally stay overnight in her apartment (she was now living on her own). I was still living at home at this time and my very blue-nosed Southern Baptist parents were well aware of where I was going and what I was doing. They did not approve. They liked Katrina just fine and grew to love her very much, but they were afraid that I was falling in love, not with the love of my life, but with the first steady sex partner I had ever had. And, unfortunately, they were right.

My friend Kim Lemser, the Vietnam veteran, had told me several years earlier about farm boys shipped off to 'Nam who had never been with a girl. When they finally got their first taste of female flesh, they immediately fell head over heels in love with their Vietnamese prostitutes and proposed marriage, which many of the girls were only too happy to accept. Of course I couldn't see myself in a parallel situation at all and was shocked when my brother told me of my parents' worries.

There was no question Katrina and I were in love. We were inseparable. But it was equally true that although neither of us, technically, were virgins, we might as well have been so little and tentative had been our previous experiences. In the lovemaking department there were many things we just simply didn't know or how to do them if we did. After the new wore off after we had married we weren't exactly burning it up under the covers.

I am a passionate person. Passionate about virtually every-thing I do and in my youthful years my libido was locked into permanent overdrive. To quote Richard Pryor, if I wasn't horny I had to check to see if my heart was beating. Not every couple is a perfect match in the boudoir. We weren't. Katrina showed more passion when she wanted to get pregnant than at any other time in our marriage. I was only too happy to oblige.

When our daughter Marie was born, as happens with everyone, the family dynamic changed. The center of our attention was Marie; our family threesome bonded and we found a love supreme that to Katrina and me trumped our difficulties between the sheets. As disappointing as intimacy had become, I confess that I was happy, happy and contented in a way I haven't been since. Today I occasionally have dreams where our family is back together again, doing family things, finding simple joy in the company of one another. I miss those days.

The Corporate Life

KATRINA, UNLIKE ME, HAD a very stable and lucrative career working in the cardiology department of a major Memphis Catholic hospital. She started her profession while a college student working part-time doing EKG hookups. This worked its way into her doing treadmills, where heart patients put stress on their hearts while walking on a tread-mill and then the heart is tested ultrasonically to see if the heart reacts abnormally to the stress. She was fascinated with the mechanics of the human heart and studied hard and diligently. She began training as an ultrasound technician which launched her into a much higher salary with greater prestige in the hospital hierarchy. Her job was the financial anchor during our entire marriage.

My jobs were much iffier propositions. Even before I had graduated from Memphis State University with a degree in Journalism my writing had been recognized and I had won some awards. I was quickly hired out of college by one of the city's better advertising agencies and put to work as a P.R. writer with a nominal salary and virtually no training or help at all. Other than part-time college jobs I had no real experience in the corporate world and almost immediately discovered myself a very square peg in a very round hole. I never took to the cubicle life and found the typical 8 to 5 routine oppressive and life-diminishing. Looking back, I don't think there is a single boss I ever liked. With my flinty attitude it is no wonder that despite appreciation for my writing talents, I was forever in hot water over one thing or another, sometimes just chickenshit demerits like lingering too long over coffee breaks and sometimes when I'd clearly crossed the lines of corporate etiquette. I blame myself.

My advertising work won awards, lots of them, but I wasn't liked in the high offices due to my abrasive personality. Outside the office, people thought I was a friendly and affable fellow. Inside I was thorny and combative. The reason was simple enough; I hated what I was doing.

The longest and best job I had during this period of my life was as the copywriter for a major manufacturer of orthopedic and otology devices, Richards Medical Company. It paid well and I worked with a great group of talented creative people. I even liked my boss most of the time. I lasted there nearly seven years, a record, until I began teaching.

*   *   *

One of my favorite characters at Richards Medical Company was Dr. Hugh Smith, a retired super-surgeon who was hired as the medical consultant for the company. Dr. Smith was without question one of the ten greatest orthopedic (Dr. Smith made a point of spelling the word "orthopaedic") surgeons of the 20th Century and even after retiring from surgery in 1982 was much in demand as a consultant all over the world. His official title at Richards Medical Company was chief medical officer. I was the chief copywriter for the company, a much lower position let me assure you, writing ads that appeared in orthopedic journals as well as surgical techniques that step-by-demanding-step told surgeons how to perform new surgeries.

Dr. Smith reviewed every word I wrote and often laid into it with a heavy red pen. On my bookshelf today rests a paperback copy of the indispensable writers' reference book *Elements of Style* by Strunk and White signed by "the old weird orthopod, Hugh Smith." I think he hoped his little gift would improve my writing.

Dr. Smith, in his retirement years, was known to take a

drink or two, often before the socially acceptable hour of 5 p.m. One afternoon, Dr. Smith and I were waiting for a flight with a group of others from Richards Medical Company.

"What do you bet some big, fat nigger woman comes and sits right next to me on this plane?" Dr. Smith cackled into my ear at the airport that day, the tang of bourbon perfuming his breath.

Well, what does an underling say to that?

Dr. Smith was known for salty language and wasn't exactly careful with his racial rhetoric either. So, was this man a racist? Based upon such alcohol-fueled utterances one could be forgiven for thinking so.

But like almost everything in Memphis involving race, not all was as simple as black and white. I can clearly remember a Christmas ceremony at Richards Medical when Dr. Smith, a concert level organist who often gave recitals on the city's grand pipe organs, performed an organ duet with a black employee who was an organist for his church. The gospel style of the black church and Dr. Smith's classical leanings meshed wonderfully. At the finish Dr. Smith gave a slight smile, a flourish of his hands on the keyboard as he hit the final notes, and there was a noticeable twinkle in his eye.

Dr. Smith was one of the founding surgeons of the world-renowned Campbell Clinic. He was an editor and writer for several editions of *Campbell's Operative Orthopaedics*, which is the bible of orthopedics, a tome directly responsible for the healing of millions upon millions of broken bones. As Dr. Smith would tell me, a great deal of orthopedic learning was advanced by war, particularly World War II. Soldiers needing bone treatment were sent via train to Memphis and Kennedy Hospital, which proved to be a training ground for Campbell Clinic surgeons and their interns.

On September 26, 1937, when Dr. Smith was still an intern at Campbell Clinic and destined to become one of the greatest surgeons in his field, he had set off with a fishing buddy shortly after midnight, heading down the fabled Highway 61 into Mississippi, most likely wanting to get an early start on the fish biting at Tunica Lake. Around 2 a.m. he came upon a terrible automobile accident. A black man and woman had sideswiped a heavy truck that had pulled in front of them as it tried to re-enter the highway having been pulled over on the shoulder. The impact of the collision sheared off the woman's arm below her elbow and had severely damaged her internal organs. According to an interview with Dr. Smith years later what he witnessed was "a traumatic amputation." Dr. Smith was a take charge kind of man, a leader, a general among surgeons. Even as an intern he had undoubtedly treated thousands of African-Americans. I know this for fact because he regaled me with stories about treating black patients. And no, these weren't racist stories. Just a doctor's tales, and he had seen a lot.

At first, Dr. Smith did not know that the woman who was almost bled-out lying in the middle of Highway 61 was the blues diva Bessie Smith. Even though he was an avid fisherman who probably felt some irritation that his fishing recreation was going to be delayed, he nonetheless prepared and applied a tourniquet to Bessie Smith, trying to keep her from completely bleeding to death. His fishing buddy ran to get help from a nearby farmhouse. Dr. Smith began to clean his car out to make room to transport Bessie Smith and her driver to the nearest black hospital which was located not even half a mile from the white hospital, which everyone thereabouts knew did not accept black patients. That was a sad fact of life in 1937 in the heart of the Mississippi Delta.

Just as Dr. Smith threw some things by the side of the road to make room in his car for Bessie Smith, a car driven by two whites plowed into the back of his vehicle, slamming it into Bessie Smith's car. Suddenly Dr. Smith had four people injured on the highway, not two. Ambulances arrived soon after. One of them, driven by a black man, took Bessie Smith directly to the nearby black hospital, the G.T. Thomas Afro-American Hospital, in Clarksdale. (The hospital was converted to a hotel, The Riverside, in 1944 and virtually every blues musician of note at one time or another stayed there. Today it is a major tourist attraction in the city.) Within a few hours after admission to the hospital Bessie Smith, the reigning blues queen of the 1920s whose fame had all but dissipated by 1937, was dead. She was to perform the next day in Darling, Mississippi and had left Memphis earlier that evening. Dr. Smith told an interviewer in 1938 and a Bessie Smith biographer decades later that there was virtually no chance of Bessie Smith surviving such a traumatic accident. I believe him.

Just as with blues legend Robert Johnson who I have written about, a whole myth has grown about Bessie Smith and her death on Highway 61. The most prominent of the tales is that Bessie Smith died because she was refused admission to the white hospital. It never happened. No one in 1937 would have wasted one minute trying to take her there. Especially with a black hospital practically right next door. Another of the conjectures is that Dr. Smith could have saved Bessie's life but refused to touch her because she was black. Yet another has it that he didn't want to get his car bloody by transporting her to the hospital. The facts are that Dr. Smith—the same man who whispered those shocking words in my ear—stepped up and did everything he could to save Bessie Smith and in the process had his Chevrolet automobile totaled and his holiday ruined.

With his own hands there is no question in my mind that Dr. Smith saved thousands of lives of whites, blacks, and numerous other races. His innovative and progressive ortho-pedic surgeries, not to mention instruments and implants he invented, plus his work on the all-important *Campbell's Operative Orthopaedics*, saved and healed millions. I have been treated for injuries at Campbell Clinic several times in my own life, since I was a teenager falling off a skateboard. Residents of Memphis consider it the best orthopedic hospital in the world. So do many others. Dr. Smith's techniques very probably were used to heal me.

I never knew that Dr. Smith was the one who stopped that early morning on Highway 61 to tend to Bessie Smith. Had I known, I would have plied the doctor with endless questions, probably to his annoyance. He said some bad things, yes, made some very off-color remarks, certainly. Yet his actions showed that he was a man fully capable of putting those Jim Crow-era feelings in an interior jack-in-the-box that would spring open only when he was good and ready and felt you were the right audience. As the Good Book says, we are sinners all. Dr. Smith, in my estimation, was a great man, quite eccentric, quite brilliant, and if you were around him you never knew what he might say. That old weird orthopod; I'm glad to have known him and even with his dark flashes think he did the world a hell of a lot more good than evil. Rest in peace, Hugh Smith.

Beyond the Comfort Zone

THE AD AND P.R. world is volatile under the best of circumstances, but even when I behaved myself to the best of my abilities my loathing for that world would eventually out itself and I'd be pounding the pavement again looking for another job.

This certainly tried the patience of my rock steady wife, Katrina. Our marriage had settled into a comfort not unlike a favorite pair of broken-in house slippers. Romance was infrequent and not terribly exciting, but we traveled, we went every weekend to the cinema, we delighted in the new thing called cable TV and the HBO channel and MTV that came with it. We ate out at Memphis' best restaurants and especially loved finding little holes in the wall that served great food. We were foodies long before I'd ever heard the term.

Katrina's family was special to me as well. Her mother was one of those well-mannered and gracious Southern ladies who always had a hug, a big smile, and a wink for everyone. Oh my, was she a good cook. Katrina's father was the child of Italian immigrants and was an Army Ranger who scaled the cliffs on Normandy Beach during D-Day. He was captured by the Germans and spent the rest of the war in Dresden, where Kurt Vonnegut also was imprisoned. Tudy, his nickname, was a wonderful character, a trove of great stories, most of which were played for laughs. I loved both of my in-laws.

Katrina's older sister, Judy, was her best friend. She did not like to invite anyone else but her sister and a few old high school pals into her narrow circle. Even today, Katrina and Judy can be counted on to be out shopping together every weekend. They are never far apart. At family events and gatherings it is inevitable that the two will sit next to one another and chat amongst themselves virtually the whole time they are there.

I am the complete opposite when it comes to friends. I am wide open to let any interesting person into my life. It is not uncommon for me to meet someone at a party, exchange business cards, and bring them into my circle. This would be impossible with Katrina.

Her closeness to her sister Judy felt like a noose to me that kept getting tighter and tighter. Judy's husband, a hard-drinking ne'er-do-well, after a long day of drinking and then driving home so drunk he had to be helped to bed, fell down a flight of stairs and hit his head, killing him instantly. With him gone, Judy and Katrina clung together all the more tightly. And so they remain.

The birth of Marie altered our universe. From birth Marie was beautiful, highly intelligent, and charming. She loved everyone and everyone loved her right back. Although Katrina and I did not go to church, we allowed my mother to take Marie to Sunday School when she was kindergarten age.

We figured that exposing Marie to her grandmother's religion would be educational for her and she could see what other people did on Sundays. Marie became a favorite of the seniors at my Mom's church and she would come home with a pocket full of candy treats they had brought for her.

Marie was a self-disciplined child as she grew up. Other than an occasional mild scolding she didn't need any correction. She was a delight to be around and said so many clever things about life and the world around her that I wish we had written them all down. Our family was full of hugs and kisses and bedtime stories and movie time. Marie was so well-behaved that she got constant invitations from other parents and grandparents for sleepovers with their children and grandchildren. They all thought Marie was a good influence.

Katrina was a deep sleeper who would not wake up even during storms or someone ringing our doorbell in the middle of the night. I wake up at the slightest noise. When Marie was about five years old I woke up one night with Marie standing in our bedroom like some sort of apparition looking at us silently. After jumping out of my skin I collected myself and demanded to know what was the matter. She answered by running back to her bed bawling. I had no idea what had prompted this. Was she sleepwalking? The next day I told Katrina what had happened. After quizzing Marie again, we still were no closer to what had happened.

Then a few nights later, it happened again. I told Marie to go back to bed. She ran crying again. This continued off and on for about a month until Katrina figured out the problem. We had decorated Marie's room with all manner of childhood bric-a-brac from Beatrix Potter figurines to Mardi Gras masks hanging merrily on the wall. The masks were the problem. To Marie, when the lights were turned down those happy faces began to take on sinister and scary overtones. As she lay in bed she thought those distorted clown faces were staring at her, waiting, waiting to do evil things if she slipped into sleep.

Katrina took away all the masks and no human or animal figures were left in the room. Problem solved.

Marie got excellent grades, loved books, and was exceptionally good in math, my Achilles' heel in school. Although she loved to play with other children and even today is about as social as a person can be, she never took much interest in extra-curricular activities. She had no interest in soccer, Brownie Scouts, softball, or sports of any kind. Katrina wanted Marie to learn ballet, and because at that time I was freelancing from our house, I was the one designated to take her to dance class. I was the only man there. The housewives would sit and gossip as I sat by myself, reading or doing work of one sort or another.

From down the hall I kept hearing the dance teacher: "Marie, join the rest of us." "Marie, honey, let's put the toys down and get in the group." "Marie, please don't climb up on the radiator. You might hurt yourself."

After peeking in the classroom one day and seeing Marie staring out the window and not participating in the dance exercises at all I decided that I'd had enough of ballet and ended Marie's only foray into the dance arts.

Marie knew I was a writer and later vaguely she understood I was the editor of a magazine *(Rock & Roll Disc)* and worked with lots of writers. She pretty much ignored my world of letters and my love of rock music and electric guitars, the latter of which she pretty much loathed. (Today her husband, like me, plays guitar and Marie still hates it.)

As unhappy as I was with parts of my marriage, day-to-day life was steady on and for the most part pleasant and comfortable. I placed a lot of value on comfort and do today. As Marie grew up life as a family unit was almost idyllic. We were close and worked out our problems together. One of her teachers in an early grade had gotten me off to the side one day and cautioned me that Marie was showing too much interest in the boys. Privately I scoffed at this; my Dad had been told the exact same thing about me with girls when I was in grade school and he dismissed it as an old maid's ditherings.

When Marie was in middle school she came in one day and as usual I greeted her and asked, "How was school today?"

She had an odd look on her face and answered, "Not so good."

I said, "Why, what happened?"

She sat down next to me, buried her face in my shoulder and cried.

"A black girl in my class was running track today with us during P.E. and she fell down and had a heart attack and died."

Marie was very shaken about this and I did my best as a father to console her. Our family grieved over this little girl, who lived in a rural part of the county in a small shack-like house, and indeed the whole community mourned. The girl had a known heart condition but she was considered to be in good enough health to be able to join the other girls in the physical education class. No one tried to affix any blame to the school or school system; it was just one of those sad things in life that no one can predict and makes one question life and God when a young person with a life ahead of them is taken out with no warning.

As I worried about Marie during this time, I could not help but reflect on how little difference it made to my daughter that this little girl was black. Her race just didn't matter. We sent a sympathy card to the family. They had a memorial service at her school for the girl. How different were things then compared to the day I saw the first black student who integrated Bethel Grove school. And as I write this I think about the wake I recently attended of a precious little black lady, Darlene Hicks, who worked at the college where I teach, LeMoyne-Owen, as a staff administrator who also took one of my adult classes that were held on Saturdays. She was such an eager learner and expressed such excitement over the material we covered. She had to drop out of my class due to health concerns, but occasionally she would visit and we would always hug and catch up on news with one another.

I had seen Darlene at another funeral only weeks before she passed. She was entering the building using a walker but she was glad to see me and as always we hugged and talked for a bit. Then she died. I do not like going to funerals or wakes and hers was to be held in the town of Millington on the far outskirts of Memphis, which made the trip even more onerous to me. But I felt I had to go.

Using my GPS, I drove down miles of winding country roads until I could see what appeared to be a long line of cars parked alongside the road. I could see a tiny church up a road grade and knew this had to be the place. Slotting my car between two others, I walked several hundred yards on the side of the road and slowly climbed a long gravel drive until I reached the front of the country church. Inside, the room was totally packed, most people in their Sunday best. Only a handful of whites were in attendance, but I have no doubt that everyone in the room knew instantly that I was a professor at LeMoyne-Owen College there to pay my respects. Her daughters knew me and walked to greet me. I do not like to view the deceased lying in their coffins. Since I was very young seeing dead people has thoroughly creeped me out. I go to great lengths to avoid it. But Darlene was lying in a white coffin right dead smack in the middle of the room and looking at her was unavoidable.

As I peered down through a white gauze spread over her, she looked like an angel, as lovely as I had ever seen her, and so at peace that I felt an instant calm, as if she and I were walking hand in hand in the spirit world.

I have mentioned that I am not a religious person. But I have learned from the black culture that I was raised in and my time in Africa not to ever dismiss the spirit world that virtually every black person I've ever known—whether in the U.S. or in Africa—believes in or to cynically laugh off the feelings I experience in such situations. I totally felt I connected in some spiritual way as I looked down at this precious student who made teaching so very real to me.

As I drove back home that night I felt an elation, as if my soul had been cleansed, that I had in some way been touched by the hand of God. The same God I sometimes have a hard time believing in.

When people ask me on occasion what I believe in I tell them, "I don't know."

Because I don't.

My head tells me one thing and my heart tells me something else. I've learned to live with that and not question it.

The Life and Death
of Kenneth Williamson

Untitled painting by Kenneth Williamson

IN MY CHILDHOOD MY parents seldom went on vacations or drove cross country. Most car trips were back to their hometown of Pine Bluff, Arkansas to visit our many relatives who never left. Because we lived in Memphis 160 miles away, our family was more or less out of the loop of the rest of our extended family and we were subtly treated as outsiders, but outsiders who clearly fascinated them with our big city ways and our faster, brogue-ish Memphis accents.

To get to Pine Bluff required driving through Memphis on

Lamar Avenue, also known as Highway 78, where as children my brother and I got a bird's eye view of how the other half lived. We would pass block after block of unloved, blemished tenement buildings, black folks sitting out on lawn chairs on the landings, fanning themselves in the heat of the summer, smoke curling from under barbecue grills set up on practically every floor. Little girls in pigtails and little boys with no shirts on chased each other with playsticks, bouncing balls, running hither and yon, laughing, jumping and having their summer fun, the older girls just lounging around and trying their level best to look cool. I loved to watch them sashay together down the sidewalks, moving slowly and languidly in the heat, their hips doing a tick-tock in rhythm with their ever-present music. Many times I wished I could join in on their fun. Even when very small I understood that these people were poor and did not have some of the nice things I did. To this day I equate apartment living with being poor. I once visited the controversial author Albert Goldman in his Central Park West apartment, one of the most valuable real estate properties in the world. When I left I thought to myself, "Hell, my apartment in Memphis is *lots* nicer than that."

As the Graves family crossed the brown, rapidly-flowing Mississippi River into the flat bottomlands of East Arkansas we were quickly removed to a more forlorn, desolate world, observing poverty first hand. In those days there were hundreds of tar paper shacks dotting the farmlands along the highway, black families toiling in their yards, washing machines from a bygone era often doing their duty, sitting on sagging front porches, occasionally a large black cauldron boiling away in the front yard used to wash white laundry. Countless times I saw one of the last vestiges of the plantation era—families picking cotton during the fall harvest, bodies bent double dragging large sacks filled with cotton behind them, hand-picking the cotton bolls and moving up the row, children picking as well as the elderly, everyone pitching in to get the crop in. Those cotton dollars during a good season paid for food and clothes for the whole next year.

At that age I had never done a hard day's labor in my life. In fact my parents sheltered my brother and me from hard work probably because they had seen too much of it in their own childhoods. My one chore was taking out the garbage. Mom didn't trust us to do the dishes or clean the house; she did those things her own way. Dad wouldn't let us wash the car or cut the grass until we were older; he did those things his own way. Watching those families picking cotton looked very inviting to a white child who didn't have a clue as to the sweat and misery behind a day of picking cotton in the hot sun. Like many such whites, I romanticized those scenes in my mind, always thinking pleasant thoughts when reminiscing about those country drives during my youth. By the time I was a teenager I saw less and less of the cotton picking in Arkansas. It was by then a thing of the past. Mechanization and big agri-business had taken over.

In the 1980s my wife, Katrina, and I were shopping at Memphis' Greatest Store, Goldsmith's, which is now a Macy's. Katrina was an Art History major in college and was attracted to all kinds of art, particularly some of the local artists, many of whom specialized in watercolor painting. One local artist she and many others sought out was Dolph Smith whose rustic Southern barn and wooden shack paintings were much in demand. Such scenes had long been a very tired trope among Southern artists, but Smith was a very inventive colorist, adding unfamiliar and curious hues to what otherwise would have been quite ordinary images. His work far transcended the usual.

That day at Goldsmith's Katrina and I were both struck by a painting by an artist named Kenneth Williamson, a name we did not know. It was a signed and numbered print and the scene was a slightly abstract watercolor of a black family picking cotton. The influence of Dolph Smith seemed to us obvious and, further, there also seemed to be an influence by another famed regional artist, Carroll Cloar. The painting exceeded our humble budget, but Katrina put it on credit and carried it home, where it still has a place of prominence in her home in the suburbs of Memphis. She also has a print by Dolph Smith and an original painting of his we bought at a yard sale, an unbelievable find.

Perhaps Kenneth Williamson's painting appealed to some wrongheaded notion of the antebellum South, the "darkies" out picking cotton, ah the good ol' days. It certainly appealed to the memories I had of driving through East Arkansas as our '58 Buick sailed through the Delta flatlands. Reading the local newspaper we learned that the artist, Kenneth Williamson, was an up-and-coming award-winning African-American watercolorist, noted for winning a Memphis in May International Festival poster contest where the honored country of that year happened to be England. Williamson had impressed everyone with his beautiful rendering of the London skyline situated along the Mississippi River. A few nobs had complained that Big Ben was in the wrong position, or some such nonsense, but no one else, including the visiting British dignitaries, cared.

Not long after, I was driving down the 1-240 expressway and noticed a huge billboard advertising one of Kenneth Williamson's paintings. To my knowledge it is the only time in Memphis history that an artist has leased his own billboard to advertise his work. Such advertising does not come cheap.

Months went by and to our horror the morning paper revealed that a man had been found dead in Martin Luther King Jr. Park down by the Mississippi River, wrapped in two sleeping bags with a single gunshot to his head. This was a professional hit, and the body being left in a public park, wrapped in sleeping bags, and with a single fatal shot to the head was meant to send someone a clear message and warning. These people were not playing.

The dead man was Kenneth Williamson. To the surprise of no one, the murderers were never found or identified in any way. Today it is still officially a "cold case." I wasn't satisfied with what little had been written about the murder in our local papers. I wanted to know more and I thought if the story were compelling enough I might want to write about it. So, I made a few calls to contacts I had in the Memphis Police Department and made an appointment with the homicide detective in charge of the case, John Wilburn.

Homicide detectives are naturally wary of writers they don't know wanting information on a murder case, but I have a way of putting such people at ease and Det. John Wilburn wound up telling me a whole lot of things that never made it to the local papers.

Williamson, according to Det. Wilburn, was little more than a con man. He hustled people for expensive jewelry and expensive cars and used his very real artistic talents to secure funding to create public artworks for several municipalities and then absconded with the money, never lifting a finger to do the work for which he was paid handsomely. There were warrants out for him when he was found in Martin Luther King Jr. Park.

He was elevated to prominence in the black community by marrying into one of the city's most regal and celebrated black families, the Sugarmons. He also seemed to flash a lot of money around, far beyond the typical lifestyle of even the most esteemed regional artists. The reason is because he was a drug mule, according to Det. Wilburn, for a notorious clan in Memphis. Apparently Williamson somehow got crossways with the wrong person in the highly regimented regional drug trade and paid for it with his life. When the hit was put out on Williamson, it would have been very easy for him to just disappear and never be found. But the dumping of the body in the park and the single shot to the head spelled it out clearly to those in the know—*fuck with us and see what happens.*

I have run across several people in the intervening years who knew Williamson, some who knew him well. Very few will talk about him. His murder still scares a lot of people.

But in the white Memphis suburb of Cordova a painting of a black family picking cotton still hangs proudly on the wall of a den that could be featured in *Better Homes and Gardens* magazine. The painting still has the flavor of the Old South and the feeling of things the way they used to was. Seeing it today I wonder why Williamson decided to make a black family picking cotton his subject. Did he do it purposely to appeal to whites longing for the plantation era South? Was it just a cynical move to gain reputation? Or did it come from his own upbringing somewhere in the Deep South?

It's a cold case and no one has done any talking in a very long time. And I haven't seen a family picking cotton in over fifty years. Life moves on.

Free-Falling

AS MARIE ENTERED HIGH school I had taken a huge detour in my professional life. I had given up on commercial writing and turned my back on a lucrative if highly stressful career in public relations and advertising. I wanted to devote myself to my creative writing and knew I'd have to find a better day job that would enable me to do that. Several of my friends in academia encouraged me to go back to school to earn an M.F.A. degree in Creative Writing. With such a degree and my already extensive publishing record, I could surely find a full-time college teaching gig and spend my summers and other spare time writing whatever I wanted. This sounded like a wonderful plan, and I bit.

Although Katrina fully endorsed this decision, it would soon put a strain on our financial responsibilities. Katrina was highly-paid as an echocardiography technician and throughout our marriage had been the primary breadwinner. This was a sore spot with her and I can't say I blame her. She surely felt like she was funding my many follies, and over our 23 years together I had quite a few. While going back to graduate school at the advanced age of 41, I would be earning a monthly stipend to teach, but really it wasn't enough to make me much of a contributor to the family coffers. The flame of romance at this point was almost entirely blown out. As an older and far more experienced writer than the twenty-somethings in the M.F.A. program at the University of Memphis, I received my share of snubs from unimpressed fellow students and at the same time some unexpected attention from some of the coeds.

A problem for both Katrina and myself is that we both began to put on weight after we married, a common enough occurrence in the land of diabetes and heart disease. I had gained some abdominal fat, giving me a paunch, and Katrina had filled out as well. We would sling playful jibes at each other about our weight, but those jibes hurt, for me certainly and I'm sure Katrina too. I had been skinny my whole life and was hypersensitive about my weight gain. Such joking made me feel unattractive and invisible to the opposite sex, and with the stasis in the bedroom I was utterly sexually miserable— year after year.

Attention in the bedroom had reached new lows. I discovered to my surprise that not every female I came into contact with at the University of Memphis thought I was quite so undesirable. The problems in our relationship began to accelerate once I began graduate school. I published my first book, the novel *Pullers*, while still a grad student. The book had gotten a great deal of positive local coverage and a rave review in *The Washington Post*. I also had spent a month at the exclusive Bennington College in Vermont one summer at their acclaimed writers' workshop. I met many famous writers during that month—George Garrett, Thomas M. Disch, Rick Moody, Lucy Grealy, and others. My novel *Pullers* was the hit of that workshop. As one fellow attendee put it, "Tom, you are the poster boy for Bennington this year."

Several ladies at Bennington cast an eye upon me. One day in my dorm while working on a piece of writing there was a knock on my door. A young woman nearly a decade younger than me if not more was standing there with a wry smile on her face and a raised eyebrow waiting to be invited into my spare chambers. I provided that courtesy and we chatted about this and that, me not wanting to take advantage of an obvious situation. The desire was there but the heart was just not willing at this point. A few years later and I would have gloried in this moment. This was a heady time for me professionally and personally but the death knell for my marriage rang louder week by week.

I had kept on the straight and narrow during my marriage despite such temptations as described and my closet wish— oh, how I prayed—was for at least one more sex partner in my lifetime. During a moment of high frustration with Katrina in the bedroom, I told her I was giving up on sex with her. Enough was enough. I told her not to question any late nights out at that point. After that we were never to be intimate again.

The marriage rapidly eroded at this point and when we announced to Marie that we would be breaking up, she was in shock. She didn't see any of it coming. Since I would be the one leaving, she naturally thought I was the one breaking up the family and for a long time she kept her distance from me, which hurt more than anything else during this period of my life. I have been told by many others who are well-acquainted with divorce that such behavior with one's children is well-established. When the father moves out, an automatic wall is erected between him and his children no matter how blameless the separation. When I left and lived on my own in a small apartment and began seeing other women undoubtedly it looked to Marie as if I were cheating on her Mom. This took a painfully long time to heal and it was only years later that I wanted Marie to know the whole truth about why I left Katrina.

Even the most amicable of divorces takes a toll. I was no exception. For some time afterwards I felt I was in a state of free-fall; nothing seemed to be settled, no direction the right one. I had graduated from the University of Memphis with my M.F.A. in Creative Writing, the university's first student to specialize in Creative Nonfiction. I had published my first book, *Pullers*, which surprised even my closest friends by being fiction rather than nonfiction. I've always had a restless muse and I never know just where my interests will lead me. At that time I was best known as a music writer, having edited *Rock & Roll Disc* magazine and written music-related reviews and articles for *Rolling Stone, Musician, The New York Times*, and in particular *The Washington Post*. But I had never just stuck with one thing. I am convinced that if I had continued with a series of tough Grit Lit fiction like my novel *Pullers*, I would be better known in literary circles today.

But it was eight years before I was to publish a second

book, *Crossroads: The Life and Afterlife of Blues Legend Robert Johnson*, which is by far my best known work and which won an award for best literature book of 2011 from the prestigious Blues Foundation. As of 2019 it has been published in four languages. Oddly, it was my ex-wife Katrina who spurred me into action writing this book. Katrina and I have remained friendly since our divorce and chat every couple of months or so and, of course, see each other at family celebrations. One of the things I like about Katrina is that she tells it like it is; she doesn't dance around.

During a telephone chat I said something about being "an author" and she chuffed, "Why do you keep calling yourself 'an author'? You haven't written anything in, what, ten years now?"

My feeble retort was, "Ha. It's only been eight years."

She's always known how to plant what I call smart bombs that don't do their full damage until days later. Well, this off-hand comment really got to me, and the reason is because it was so true.

My goal in life had been to publish a book with my name on the spine. I had reviews and articles and essays published in book anthologies and compilations, but I wanted a book that was all mine. *Pullers* accomplished that. But then another worry set in; would I be one of those people who published just one book, a one-hit wonder so to speak?

Shortly thereafter, I was sitting in the auditorium of Hickory Ridge Middle School in a black part of town for a Black History Month presentation. Students, each holding a big letter of the alphabet, came out on the stage and for every letter recited a passage about a famous African-American whose last name began with the letter of the alphabet they held. "A" was Muhammad Ali. "X" was Malcolm X. When they got to the letter "J" I kept thinking Robert Johnson, Robert Johnson, but it turned out to be for Jesse Jackson, a worthy enough figure, for sure, but not one to whet my imagination.

This got me to thinking: there is no biography of Robert Johnson for high school age students. Hmmm, that would require about 100 pages of manuscript and I could easily knock that out in a semester using available source materials, or so I thought. I quickly discovered that much to my surprise there was very little reliable information extant about Robert Johnson. The articles and book entries about him mostly recycled the same hackneyed stories and I simply could not believe the lack of diligence in research. How bad was it? Greil Marcus, one of the most esteemed of music writers, in his classic book *Mystery Train* in the chapter on Robert Johnson consistently misspells Johnson's birthplace of Hazlehurst, Mississippi as Hazelhurst. This mistake, admittedly minor, is in at least seven and counting editions of the book. No one has bothered to date to correct it. It was widely reported— part of the legend, in fact—that Robert Johnson died from strychnine poisoning. But no researcher, not a single one, had bothered to investigate this type of poisoning. I suspected that as a cause of death, being poisoned with strychnine was highly unlikely and could not have been easy to pull off. Experts on poisoning that I consulted confirmed my conclusion. They agreed with me that it was much more likely Robert Johnson died from tainted moonshine, which was common enough during the Depression era.

After writing the first page of the book, it was no longer a book for children. It was a fully adult book and I never looked back. A year later *Crossroads* was published and it received glowing reviews in the music press and a thumbs up from the notoriously critical blues cognoscenti. I owe it all to Katrina.

After getting my M.F.A. and publishing my first book I became an adjunct professor, teaching at several area colleges. Although Memphis is a large metropolitan area, there are relatively few colleges and universities with full-time openings for a Creative Writing instructor. The University of Memphis as a matter of policy does not hire its own graduates for tenure-track positions. So, I took whatever teaching job I could get and scraped by living in the garage apartment, formerly servants' quarters, behind the large Midtown home of an old friend.

As stated previously, I made up my mind to be bold and assertive when it came to the opposite sex and shrug off rejection, which in my youthful days would crush my spirit. I began to date furiously and had a grand time doing it. I fell into an ill-advised relationship shortly after my divorce with a Journalism co-ed I had panted after for many years when I was an undergraduate. She was smart, fun, could have made a good writer had she pursued it, was fearless and imaginative in the lovemaking department, and severely alcoholic, which at first she kept well hidden from me. The deeper the relationship got, the crazier and more chaotic the nights became. She was clingy, whiny, and unstable, and I began to suffocate. I ended things and began dating someone else; my tires were slashed. You do the math.

Later that year I met a stunning blonde, a thirty-some-thing-year-old student who was going back to school to finish her bachelor's degree. Up to that point in my life she was unquestionably the most beautiful woman I had ever been with. I was very proud to be seen with her around town—until she opened her pretty mouth and no telling what melange of nonsense would come out. I do not like drugs. I do not like excessive use of alcohol. I cannot stand potheads. She claimed she had carpal tunnel syndrome and was trying every which way to wangle disability from Social Security. She also claimed several other ailments and smoked a cumulonimbus or two of pot every day to ward off these mystery pains. That rank smell of high-dollar marijuana trailed her like a lost puppy. She reeked of it.

She was forever broke and loved the fact that I had cable television. I have noticed that marijuana-benumbed slackers like nothing better than to channel surf for hours on end. She would occupy the remote control until the sun rose and then sleep until I came home from work in the evening. This situation did not last long—how could it?—and it taught me an important lesson about chasing the most beautiful girl in the room. Namely, what do you do after you catch her?

All this time something else was happening. As I availed myself of the bars, nightclubs, and gathering spots around town, I seemed to be catching the eye of some magnificent-looking black women. Which took me back to my earlier years working at First National Bank, when I was surrounded by a bevy of brown-skinned beauties.

After my divorce with Katrina, I learned of a great blues club that was black-owned and offered the real deal—authentic, undiluted electric black blues that played to a black audience, unlike that canned Muzak blues ("Stormy Monday" anyone?) down on touristy Beale Street that wasn't fit to sit through. The club was called Wild Bill's, owned by a sweet, dapperly-dressed octogenarian who simply loved the music he had grown up with. Five dollars at the door and the music would start at 11 p.m. They sold beer by the quart and offered three food items: burgers, "wangs," fries. One dollar per *wang*. By 1 a.m. the place would be packed.

What I picked up on very quickly was that most of the blacks who came to Wild Bill's were not born in Memphis; typically they were from the Mississippi and Arkansas deltas and were country people. They grew up with blues, not the more urban sounds of Memphis soul. Also the behaviors were different. These folks seemed much more relaxed, mellow, out to have a good time, and were not interested in causing any form of mayhem. The place was friendly to all visitors and safe. Fights and tempers were not allowed and the rules were rigidly enforced by the habitues who came back week after week. It didn't take long for me to get to know people and them me. The women would literally grab you by the collar and pull you onto the dance floor. There was no way a single fella in that bar was not going to dance.

Sometimes interesting things happened out on that dance floor. Once while dancing energetically, a girl took my hands and in full view of the whole crowd placed my hands on her breasts.

"Go ahead," she commanded me.

Another girl, who informed me that in the next week she'd be getting some front teeth, began to close dance. And by close, I mean *close*. Then she began to grind. When the song was over she told me in words I won't repeat here her pleasure at my noticeable physical reaction.

Another unforgettable evening a girl looked at me and said, "You pretty, you know that?" Then she said, "I'm going to take you home with me and fuck the shit out of you."

And she did. Much, much later in the wee a.m. hours, I will never forget how we were relaxing watching an old Tarzan movie, *Tarzan's New York Adventure*.

"Cheetah drunk as a motherfucker," she commented.

Another sweet girl named Helen became very attached to me. For reasons to be explained the relationship was short-lived, but I have very fond memories of her. My takeaway memory is of her asking me for a photograph of myself. She had brought me a glamour photo of herself she had taken at a local studio, which I still have. The next time I went to her house, sitting in a place of prominence on a curio shelf in her dining room was my picture in a very elegant frame.

During this interregnum, I had my fun and did all I could to make up for 23 years of feeling unloved or at best under-loved. I don't regret a single moment or a single thing and would do it all over again if I had the chance. A few years ago a foreign visitor to Memphis who knew of my book *Crossroads: The Life and Afterlife of Blues Legend Robert Johnson* wanted to go with me to a real, authentic juke joint and I recommended Wild Bill's, which I hadn't visited in many years. I was worried that I may have lost or at least misplaced my mojo from those days when I had danced and cavorted so happily within those sweaty walls.

As soon as I walked in the door of Wild Bill's Blues Club my mojo was instantly back.

"Hey baby," said the first girl I laid eyes on, "come here and sit next to me!"

I smoothly told her and her girlfriend that I was meeting a foreign fella and we needed to catch up on things, but that I'd return later. So after my friend left a couple of hours later I sauntered over to the girls' table and asked if I could finish my drink with them before I headed home for the night.

"Sure, baby," was the response.

Before I left they asked to exchange phone numbers and I gave them my card. The pretty one with the gold-capped tooth put my card down her cleavage and into her bra and said, "You saw where I put that didn't you?"

Long live Wild Bill's.

Black Zoo

TO PARAPHRASE CHARLES DICKENS, it was the worst
of times and it was the worst of times. The year was 2000, the
new millennium was in full swing, and I was going through a
divorce after 23 years of marriage, living in a tiny garage apartment where I received few visitors, was struggling financially,
barely making ends meet as I shuttled from one class to
another as an adjunct instructor, teaching at the University of
Memphis and across the bridge and across the world in West
Memphis, Arkansas, which is about as much like Memphis as
Istanbul and a whole lot more grim. My daughter, distraught
over the divorce, all but shunned me during this period, and
I was mired in an on-the-rebound relationship that was more
stressful by far than the divorce.

I was depressed, irritable, and in no way at my best. The
glory of having a novel published in 1998 and the lines of
well-wishers at book signings was by the year 2000 but a dim
memory. In my forties I had worked hard to earn the M.F.A.
degree in Creative Writing, thinking that with my extensive
publications in notable periodicals plus my novel *Pullers*,
I wouldn't have too hard a time getting a position teaching

Creative Writing at an area college. I was wrong. Creative Writing positions are among the most contested and hotly desired of any in academia. When I was an undergraduate in the '70s I and other serious students would pay homage at one of the professor's offices just to see the framed check from *Esquire* magazine that he had gotten for an article that was accepted but never published. Getting published in a major magazine was the Holy Grail. It is what we students aspired to. Publishing a book of just about any kind at that time put you on the yellow brick road to tenure with students prostrate at your feet, a fat paycheck, long idle summers sitting on the veranda with cool drinks and deep conversation, and a 3/2 teaching load (three classes in the Fall semester, two in the Spring semester) that made being a Creative Writing professor just about the easiest and most lucrative lazy-man's job in the Western World. This is what I most desired.

But it sure wasn't what I got. Times had changed by the year 2000. Very few people could earn a steady living writing, unless you opted to whore yourself in advertising or public relations. Which is precisely what I had done after I graduated in 1976 with an undergraduate degree in Journalism. There was little alternative. I made respectable money—enough to start a family—but I hated every minute of ad and P.R. writing. After spending the day toiling over ad headlines, my cleverness stretched to its limit, I found it impossible to come home and do any serious creative writing. A few people are able to do both, people with great reserves of energy and amphetamines, but I found my creativity utterly drained by 5 p.m. every weekday and all I wanted as night approached was a good meal, a good movie or book to dig into, and quality time with my family.

After graduation in 1976, I understood almost immediately that there was a fork in the road of my life: one life led to a gainful career in a corporate office as an advertising or public relations drone, the other to a hand-to-mouth existence as a creative writer. Freelance writing couldn't produce the kind of income needed for a modest home, a modest automobile, a few minor luxuries, and a golden child. I've told my intimate acquaintances that had I loved advertising in the same way I've loved following my creative muse, I'd be earning six figures or more every year and I truly believe that.

But no matter how hard I set my nose to the grindstone, no matter how I tried to tamp down the real Tom Graves lurking inside, no matter how hard I tried to conform, blend in, be one of the gang, the walls of those cubicles locked me into a daily vise that began to squeeze the corporate-loathing monster inside of me out into plain view. Like Lon Chaney in the original *Phantom of the Opera*, I was unmasked, but I had always done my own unmasking. My "attitude" landed me sooner or later into just about every boss's office for a talking-to. Advertising and public relations being the volatile businesses they are, on more than one occasion I found myself with a pink slip, walking papers, and a boot up the ass.

My dad was afraid of almost nothing. He had been a combat veteran of World War II and grew up in the poverty belt of the South during the Great Depression and knew full well what it was like to be hungry and poor. The one thing he feared was a return to destitution. He fretted over every downturn in the economy and despised Republicans for what he perceived as a political party consumed by the rich at the expense of the working man. Unusual for a Southerner, he was a staunch union man, a proud member of the Communications Workers of America, the union that represented the workers for Ma Bell. He had been through a slog of a strike that lasted three months when I was a toddler. He was forever scarred by this and worried himself sick over every other talk of a walk-out. The irony is that after decades of worry, the only other strike in his lifetime lasted only three days and he took vacation time off, meaning he didn't lose one red cent of pay. All that worry for something that never happened.

Dad's fear of being destitute rubbed off on me. On one hand I craved the security blanket of a corporate job with its dependable salary and benefits. On the other hand I was in the wrong business—advertising and public relations—for any such stability. But after earning my M.F.A. degree in Creative Writing (there is no Ph.D. in Creative Writing. The M.F.A. is a terminal degree, like a Ph.D., higher than the M.A., and is the pinnacle for that academic specialty) I had not expected the free-fall I was going through in the year 2000. Nothing seemed to be looking up.

At some point that year I became aware of a high-paying communications job with Memphis City Schools, one of the nation's largest public school systems, and most certainly one of the largest if not *the* largest population of at-risk African-American students. The power of the zeroes attracted me enough to apply for the job. I met with the no-nonsense director of communications, Janice Crawford, who had an unnerving habit of glancing up from the papers in front of her to squint at you with a stare that seemed to go straight through. I got the feeling she was very carefully taking my measure, ticking-off a checklist in her head.

Janice was obviously highly intelligent, suspicious, and intimidating. She was one of those aging black women with a stereotypical body shape—large bosomed and with a broad bottom two ax handles wide. Although she had a delicate, measured voice it was clear to me from a host of body language cues that she was a force to be reckoned with.

Much to my surprise I got the job. The pay was more than I had ever made and to this day is the most I've ever earned. I was ecstatic and counting my days before I could move out of my small garage apartment into my own home. The work wasn't anything I hadn't handled many, many times before. There were three communications managers (writers) each of whom covered a specific section of the school system. As a need arose in my area, I dealt with the principals at those schools, but we all also worked on system-wide assignments. The job was not without stress because when bad news— such as gunplay—occurred at a school, the media were in hyperdrive and the slightest misstep on our part could paint a very damning picture of the problem-plagued inner city schools, where gangs, guns, rapes, and brutality were the norm. Everything had to be run by my boss, Janice Crawford, and she was over-protective of the school system's image, to the point of obfuscating the truth. Early on I was aware of how much the local media disliked her for her stonewalling tactics.

The job I most sweated was writing speeches for the big boss, the superintendent of Memphis City Schools, Johnny B. Watson, an African-American universally admired in Memphis. When the school system was in danger of breaking apart due to a litany of problems—fiscal mismanagement, low test scores, violence in the schools—Mr. Watson rode into office on his white horse and began to piece Humpty-Dumpty back together again. As I would learn over the years, this was Mr. Watson's specialty. He was a fixer and in my estimation one of the best. Some have argued that he wasn't a visionary, that he wasn't good at planning for the future. I think there is some truth to this, but it does not diminish the great talent he had for righting systemic wrongs.

When writing speeches for someone, by necessity it forces you to get up-close and personal. You listen to that person, you get a feel for them, the way they speak, the way they think, the way they present themselves to the public, their rhythms, their cadences. You take extensive notes on what they have on their mind and imbue it with your own thoughts that fit the topic and the event. It is very hard work, mentally exhausting, but when you hear someone deliver a rousing speech that you wrote and see how it moves a crowd, that is the payback.

Mr. Watson liked the speeches I wrote for him and word began to fly around the halls at Memphis City Schools that Tom Graves was an ace speech writer. People began to ask me to send them copies of those speeches I had written. I thought Janice, my boss, would be well-pleased. After about three or four months I noticed her taking a sharper pen to the speeches, questioning many of my comments. I never got such critiques from the big boss, Mr. Watson. I also noticed how Janice lingered over my assignments during our weekly department meetings when we reported on all of our individual tasks. A question here, a shifting of priorities there, a few rejoinders that seemed a bit pointed.

I also found out that Memphis City Schools—colloquially known as the Board of Education—was a vipers' nest of internecine intrigue. A girlfriend of mine at the time called the Board a "black zoo" and as racist as that sounds it sometimes wasn't far from the truth. I hadn't been there long enough to know who was what in terms of the gang warfare that took place right under our noses in the administration building's hallways. I found myself stumbling into all kinds of administrative punji pits just doing my job. I was assigned to do a story on a charter school located in downtown Memphis that had done an excellent job working with troubled at-risk students. I happened to know one of the leading teachers and coaches there, a Ray McGarity, who had gone to my grammar school and had lived on the street right behind mine. I got a great story from him and worked with a photographer to get a terrific photo of him working with his students.

Janice flew into a rage when I presented her with my story and photos.

"Why are you doing a story on Ray McGarity?" she stormed.

"He's leading the program at the school," I answered. "I thought that was the story I was after here."

"We can't use him," she said. "We'll have to find one of the other teachers."

And so I had to redo the entire story using a different teacher with a different photo. Why? Because Ray McGarity's wife worked in the administration building and Janice saw her as a member of a rival gang. A threat to her power.

It would get worse.

She began to dawdle over my speeches, often waiting until the final deadline loomed before demanding major changes that I had to sweat bullets to finish on time. To make matters even more difficult, her suggestions for changes often made no sense. When I would discuss them with her I would get an earful of bafflegab that as often as not left me even more puzzled.

I finished up one speech that ran me late into the afternoon and I knew she was attending the monthly meeting of the elected Board that made rulings for the school system. So, I asked her personal secretary where I should leave the speech to get her attention when she was done with her meeting. She suggested I place the document in her chair at her desk. Seemed logical to me; that's the method of delivery for important documents you want someone to make sure to see wherever I've worked.

The next morning she was all up my ass about not having gotten revisions back to her.

"Janice, I put the speech in your office chair," I said. "That's what your secretary told me I should do when I asked her."

Oh no, that wouldn't do. She told me I should have brought the speech to her right in the middle of the Board meeting, something that over months of working under her she'd never instructed me to do before. The speech went back and forth before she signed off on it just minutes before it was due.

She wrote me up for failure to produce work in a timely fashion.

I knew I was doomed when Ken Burns swanned into town. The esteemed documentary filmmaker was promoting his upcoming PBS series on jazz and part of his promotional tour involved speaking to high school musicians at special forums, often with high school jazz bands—Memphis had a good one—doing the warm-up. Much to my disappointment, Burns did not fall under my purview, but I made it known that I planned to go to the event for him and even offered to pitch in and help with any promotional effort. To that end I made calls to some of the reporters in the media I was close to who I knew would be interested in anything involving Ken Burns. This was all well-coordinated with the director in charge of Memphis City Schools' music curriculum.

On the day of the Burns event, just before I left my office, one of the secretaries from the Music Department came into the Communications Department and asked if anyone was going downtown to the Ken Burns affair. I told her I was going. She asked if I would mind taking the director of the Music Department some extra flyers he had called for. I said I would and told her I was leaving for a quick lunch and would go directly to the Burns affair afterward. All was fine.

As I lugged a small box of flyers into the auditorium I was met with several people in full panic. They had run out of flyers and the Ken Burns people were berating them for not having enough on hand. Now, you would think that I had saved the day by bringing them the extra flyers they needed. Instead I was asked why it had taken me so long. I explained that I had told the secretary I intended to get a quick bite to eat and after that I came straightaway to the event. That did not seem to suffice.

The head of the Music Department complained to my boss, Janice Crawford, that I had delayed in bringing the much-needed flyers. She not only called me into her office, but she had already written me up and put a warning notice in my employee file. I protested, explaining that all I did was try to help out and was being punished for doing a good deed. I explained that no one told me that there was any rush. Janice felt I should have assumed the importance and foregone my lunch. And there it was in cold type sitting ominously in my employee folder. The whole affair got deeply under my skin and my temper barely was in check. I left after telling Janice that next time someone asked for help, I would refuse. She glared and made a note with her pen.

The writing, as they say, was on the bulletin board. After that day, all of a sudden my speeches were terrible, my press releases not up to par, and I was further written up for minor spitting-on-the-sidewalk level offenses. I learned at the beginning of my working life that it was an absolute necessity to be on great terms with the executive secretaries wherever I happened to work. After all, they are the ones who actually run those places. I had a very good relationship with the superintendent's secretary and she was well-aware, as were many others, that I was being sandbagged by Janice Crawford. She asked me if I wanted to schedule some time with Mr. Watson. I cautiously agreed to do so. I knew I was being set up for dismissal, so what harm would there be?

My meeting with Mr. Watson, one-on-one with one of the most important CEOs in the entire Mid-South, could scarcely have gone better. Mr. Watson is a cheerful, upbeat man, but the stories I told him about Janice Crawford's behavior towards me made him visibly angry. To complicate things, I also knew there was a hiring freeze on at the Board. Despite this, Mr. Watson promised to see what he could do and counseled patience on my part.

My final run-in with Janice occurred when she ripped another of my speeches for Mr. Watson to pieces. She came into my office, shut the door behind her, and laid into me and the speech. She told me my "transitions" were terrible, claiming I was jumping from topic to topic without any connective tissue so that the speech would flow and make sense.

She looked at me dismissively and said, "Do you know what I even mean by the word 'transition'?"

I took this as a personal insult, questioning my intelligence in such a mocking, condescending way, and my temper flared.

"No, Janice, why would I know such a big word like 'transition?' I've only published one novel and several hundred articles in prominent magazines, which by the way none of you here have done. I've written how many speeches in my life? And I don't know the word 'transition.' You nailed me. I'm guilty."

My voice dripped with sarcasm, which I happen to be very good at. The thing about sarcasm is that there is no comeback to it. Janice's eyes narrowed and drilled into me. She lifted her great bulk off the seat, walked out, and never spoke a word to me again. And she fired me.

Mr. Watson and the director of human resources found a position for me to transition—there's that word again—into: there was a one-year grant for a teacher to teach 7th graders in Creative Writing. I would earn my same administrative salary for that year. After that, it would be up to the principal if he or she wanted to continue the program and whether or not he or she wanted to retain me as a teacher when I did not have the required Tennessee teaching certification to teach in a Tennessee school. In the irony of ironies I could teach college level anywhere in the country but could not teach K-12 classes without a certification, which would mean earning a whole new degree.

With only a modicum of hesitation I accepted the teaching position for one year. I was then shown the door to the third circle of hell.

A New Kind of Pain

THE SMELL OF FLOOR wax perfumed the halls of the all-new Hickory Ridge Middle School. The foyer glistened, the stately architecture was of an award-winning design. Every hand soap dispenser, every handrail, every inch of porcelain in the restrooms was unblemished, without so much as a fingerprint, smudge, or stain to defile them. The books in the library had yet to be opened, the spines uncracked. The stoves and burners in the cafeteria were yet to light a flame under their first meal.

Shortly after 8 a.m. there was a light rainfall patter of feet in the hallways. As the 8:30 bell neared the feet thundered down the hallways, a roar that had the 30 some-odd teachers in their classrooms nauseated from high nerves. The first school day began just as it would end nine months later—in a cacophony of high-decibel exhortations that would not, could not, be quieted or stilled.

I had taken on the job of teaching Creative Writing to five classes of 7th graders every weekday. These would be defined as "at-risk" students, which in real language means poor and underperforming black kids. Oh, there was a smattering of

Hispanic students and a handful of whites who were universally pitied because everyone, including their fellow students, knew they were there only because their parents were too poor to afford for them to be anywhere else. They were stuck in the pit of the Hickory Hill neighborhood, a once all-white suburb that went from white to black faster than any community I've seen in Memphis. Many people had taken to calling it "Hickory Hood" because of the high crime rate there and the blight that was eating away at still-new retail establishments along Winchester Avenue like a stage-four cancer.

In my new job there were no textbooks, no lesson plans, no instructions of any kind; I would be winging it without help from a single soul. Day by day I would have to come up with lessons and ideas to keep the students active, motivated, and in learning mode and repeat the process five times per day as one class left and another class took its place. On the first day I was as scared as if I'd been put on the front lines of a war zone, which in essence it was.

I can say without reservation that if the common citizen of Memphis knew what went on every day in the schools of this city they would burn the Board of Education to the ground. Amid the chaos and din of each and every class, learning simply cannot take place. Admittedly there are a number of black teachers who have great classroom man-agement skills and can get across a modicum of learning. Black women get more respect out of middle school students than black men because the students are used to discipline by black women. Sad to say, black men do not figure in too many of these children's lives.

If you are white, however, all bets are off. At least one-third of the teachers at Hickory Ridge Middle School were white and few had ever been in a real classroom situation on their own. They had done their student teaching for their certifications, of course, but those are sanitized events where discipline usually isn't an issue. There were no more than a handful of veteran teachers. Whites are typically seen as meek, Casper Milquetoast types, cowardly and timid when it comes to classroom control. And these 12-year-old students, as street smart as they come, run amuck with their white teachers. Later in the school year I was sent by the principal to a conference on best practices for middle school students and one of the big topics, brought up by the black teachers in attendance, was about black kids "jacking up" the white teachers. Everyone knew the white teachers were getting hell from the kids. This is what I would endure for nine more months.

I had a whole summer to prepare for my first day. As stated, the superintendent of Memphis City Schools, Johnny B. Watson, gave me the opportunity to "transition" to this grant-funded one-year position. Fearing the death spiral of unemployment, I took the job. I was sent to work that summer with the principal, whom I will call Ms. Slattery, and the white assistant principal, a once-upon-a-time Marine Corps drill sergeant, whom I will call Mr. Lane. I liked both of them, but with reservations. Ms. Slattery was someone who felt the need to put on a false front at all times; she tried her best to exude authority and let everyone know, especially arrogant men, that she was the captain of this ship. She was all-business at all times. But on the rare occasion she would let her mask down I could see a sensitive, caring, and intelligent soul who wanted little more than a comfortable life and a good book to relax with. She purposely found a home far removed from the Hickory Hill area because as she told us she didn't want to be recognized and stopped everywhere she went. She craved anonymity.

Mr. Lane, the vice principal, is the guy who warned me about what I would be up against when the school opened. Mr. Lane retained every trick from his Marine Corps days taunting new recruits. He could break down the toughest of the street kids and knew precisely how to get in their faces and scream and watch as they caved in. He was one of those Southern anomalies who is a born-again Christian, doesn't drink, smoke, or use salty language, yet is fully aware of *everything* that goes on on the Dark Side.

Because I am of a rather imposing physical stature and can talk as loud as I need to, I managed to get through my first day at Hickory Ridge, hoarse but functional. I went home wondering how in hell I would cope with what I had just gone through for nine more months. The way we eventually coped, us teachers, was by leaning on each other. We found out very quickly that we could not count on our principal, Ms. Slattery, for help. She told us she would allow the children to have candy and gum and wouldn't punish them for it. She also forbade controversial corporal punishment. Meaning she did not want the children to be paddled as most of the teachers, me included, were when they were kids. I wondered how she planned to keep control of these very wild children.

The answer was she didn't have a clue. By the end of the

first day of school, this brand spanking new building had a month's worth of scuff marks, candy wrappers, and wadded up notebook paper everywhere. Dirt and grime were on every surface. The new school was already showing age spots, frown lines, and wrinkles.

Ms. Slattery got angry with teachers like me who would march misbehaving students to her office for punishment. She cautioned me several times over the school year about sending too many students to her and about my need to learn better classroom management. When we began to put disruptive students out in the halls until class was over, she struck this from our list of disciplinary actions. The fact that she allowed candy meant that the students would load up on sweets—particularly during lunch period—and be on such a sugar high that classes after lunch were particularly difficult to control. All teachers were aware of this. The principal wasn't.

One white, middle-aged, fresh-out-of-college teacher named Robert, who I had taught at the University of Memphis as he worked towards his Education degree, came to Hickory Ridge with a broad smile and happy banter for everyone. He taught Science and could not wait to begin teaching schoolkids the rudiments of scientific discovery. His optimism was infectious. Then the bomb hit.

Robert didn't even make it until the end of the first semester. He and I and a few other teachers bonded quickly that year and would often meet out for drinks after school to let our hair down and air out our many grievances. Robert walked with a pronounced limp, the result of childhood polio which permanently altered the shape of one of his legs.

He told me with tears in his eyes about being taken from his home as a child to a polio ward where he could get the care and treatment and rehabilitation he needed, but in a sense he lost his family just as the dread disease was laying waste to him. He talked about the physical pain, the pain of losing his family, his sense of isolation, and how he would cry every night as he lay in bed, praying it would someday end and he would be reunited with his family.

But Hickory Ridge Middle School was a new kind of pain. We teachers could all see what the job was doing to Robert. This jubilant and convivial man was reduced to worry lines and a permanently furrowed brow. He began to nervously tweak his eyebrows, like Mr. Sawyer, the company psychologist in *Miracle on 34th Street*. He came to work haggard and sleepless. We worried for his health. Over drinks one afternoon he spilled to me that he was bailing out on teaching. It is rare for a teacher to quit in mid-semester and it is very frowned-upon by the powers-that-be. But Robert left and moved far, far away with his brother and planned to collect disability. And that's the last any of us heard from him.

The Mean Hamburger

IT IS GENERALLY AGREED upon by most veteran teachers that middle school students are the most difficult to teach and to keep under control. Their bodies are changing, they are undergoing puberty, their hormones are raging, and they often don't have the faintest inkling about what is happening to them. They are more temperamental, more peer-influenced, more alienated, and more sexually confused. Because of the proliferation of internet pornography, virtually all 12 and 13-year-olds have seen the whole spectrum of raw, unfiltered sex acts. But they do not know how to process it or make proper sense of it. Bringing all those unresolved emotions into the classroom presents a host of unwelcome behaviors that are a detriment to learning. Good teachers try to channel all those feelings into something productive, and I did everything I could think of to engage them and get some sort of positive interaction.

As mentioned, my Creative Writing course was an off-the-grid experiment by the Board of Education. It was based on a special government grant that funded the whole thing including my higher-than-average salary. There was no textbook extant for the course; I made it up as I went. I had to devise not only an entire curriculum, but had to figure out a way to grade the students' efforts. Any type of reading for the students required a trip to the copy room to print out—illegally—scores of copies, most of which went straight into the overflowing garbage can. I also assigned many in-class writing projects and learned that some of the students' reading skills were so poor that to call on them to read aloud their papers was a study in humiliation.

Some students openly mocked every assignment given to them; others, however, relished the opportunity to read their papers to the class, seeing the exercise as an opportunity for performance. In virtually every one of my classes there was one or two students who excelled at writing and could read their papers to the class at a near-professional level. The other students recognized this talent and were eager to hear these papers read to them and quieted down during reading time. Such events for African-American students are a communal experience; as the papers were being read there was often a collective gasp, a collective laugh, or a constant patter of commentary. White students typically sit silently until a reading is finished. Not so my students. And frankly it enlivened the whole process and made it more enjoyable for them and enlightening for me.

Occasionally I would read stories out loud, stories I thought would connect with the students. After reading these stories to five classes daily, my voice would be hoarse and sore. I had to go to an ear, nose, and throat doctor to help with the problem. The answer: drink water as I talked, which most certainly helped and is something I practice as a college professor today. I sometimes would pass out drawing paper and colored pencils and ask students to draw their impressions of a story I had read. One story in particular stands out: "The Patented Gate and the Mean Hamburger" by Robert Penn Warren. I well-remembered this story from my own high school English classes and thought it one of the most interesting stories I had ever read with a jarring ending. I wondered if it would translate well to students of the new millennium and in particular to young African-Americans.

Every class listened raptly as I read this story about a farmer and his family who loved going to town on Saturdays and eating hamburgers, which to them was the most exotically delicious food in the universe. The farmer had built a "patented gate," which was a newfangled gate that could be opened without dismounting from a horse and carriage. The farmer felt it gave him a degree of status among the local farmers, but his wife aspired to more than just farm life and had her eye on the hamburger joint. At the end of the story (spoiler alert) the farmer hangs himself from his gate and the widow sells off the farm, buys the hamburger grill, and cooks a "mean hamburger."

This story supercharged my students' imaginations and they drew all manner of impressions. Many drew human bodies with angry-looking hamburgers for heads. Several drew the farmer hanging from his gate post. A mention in the story of "tow-headed" boys resulted in several drawings of boys with big toes for heads. I put the drawings up all around the room and the students were hugely pleased with their work.

I was a fan of the short stories of Richard Bausch, who I

had met at a summer writers' retreat at the exclusive Bennington
College in Vermont. It was there I met both Bausch and his
good friend, the great George Garrett who in some ways
became a mentor to me and helped promote my first book,
the novel *Pullers*. Bausch is a master of the short story and
in middle-age was granted the great honor of a Modern
Library edition of his short stories. I can't think of an author
who writes better dialogue than Richard Bausch. One of my
favorite stories by him is "Aren't You Happy for Me?" which is
almost entirely a phone conversation between a father and his
college student daughter. The daughter is hesitantly telling her
father about a big event looming in her life. The conversation
builds to the point where the father realizes his daughter must
be pregnant. When this is revealed, the reader doesn't see it
coming and it is a surprise. As I read this to my classes, at first
I thought they were bored by the story and were lulled by my
reading. The silence, however, actually reflected how intently
they were listening. When I read out loud the possibility of
the pregnancy, the students practically jumped up and down
in their seats. But Bausch fooled us. The daughter wasn't
pregnant. She was trying to tell her father that she planned
to marry one of her professors. This stunned the father who
thought a student-professor relationship totally out of bounds.
But the big reveal, timed to perfection by Bausch, is that the
professor is sixty-five years old.

When I read this my classes—every single one—
screamed so long and loud that other teachers down the hall
came to see what was happening. They talked about this story
for *days*. I've often thought about how Richard Bausch would

have reacted to see this response to his story. I once had the honor of sitting next to Bausch in a restaurant. I asked him if the dialogue he wrote in his stories flowed naturally or if it required a lot of work and revision. Not surprisingly he told me that his dialogue, which seems so dead perfect when reading it, is the result of anguish and toil and lots and lots of editing and rewriting. The hard work shows and shows brilliantly.

Later in the school year when the results came back from the state of Tennessee's standardized tests called TCAPs, it showed that 7th grade writing skills at Hickory Ridge were higher than the reading skills by many percentage points. Seeing as how I'm not one bit shy, I told the principal point blank that I thought those higher numbers were entirely due to my teaching these kids how to write. I haven't changed my mind.

I Can't Write for You Today

BECAUSE TEACHERS GET SUMMERS off, there are
some who think teachers have it easy. Let me disabuse you
of that notion right here. Every teacher stays past the dismissal
bell. Often an armload of papers must be taken home to grade
later that night. Virtually every teacher I knew took a nap
when they got home due to utter exhaustion. I certainly did,
and it gave me a late-night boost I sorely needed. Many of these
students, just entering their teens, see the teacher as the enemy
and are out to make as much trouble in the classroom as they
possibly can. These students require constant vigilance and
discipline. Murder is in the mind of every teacher every day
of the week. At the same time, teachers are surrogate parents
for these children, many of whom come from broken and
derelict homes. Just how derelict became abundantly clear
when we started having conferences with parents. It was not
uncommon for these parents to be reeking of alcohol or weed
when they came to the school. Some mothers—fathers rarely
showed up—were dressed in such revealing clothing that we
seriously wondered if they had been plying the streets before
coming to the school. One set of parents, who were divorced,

got into such an acrimonious squabble right in front of our teacher group (the principal had divided us up into groups for the year) and their daughter that the student sat mutely with tears of shame rolling down her cheeks. Afterwards each of us teachers on our own went to the student and hugged her and told her she had nothing to be ashamed of regarding her parents' behavior. Once again we were the surrogate parents, stepping in when her own parents couldn't behave like civilized human beings. We saw this a lot.

Some 7th graders begin growing outrageously as they enter puberty. There are some girls who are every bit as filled out as grown women. Others look like little girls in pigtails playing hopscotch. The one student I will never forget was so tiny that her feet didn't touch the floor when she sat at her desk. She wore her hair in the proverbial pigtails and always wore a neatly pressed dress with bobby sox and patent leather shoes. She could have passed for a 4th grader. She never said a word in class.

Around the fourth week of the first semester, this silent student began a habit of sitting next to me before morning class began in homeroom. She was, without fail, the first student to enter the classroom every morning. I had a chair next to my desk for one-on-one conferences with students. The chair faced the classroom backwards, so the student would be facing me as we talked. I was nearly always preparing lessons or getting paperwork together in the morning as she sat next to me, but we still managed to get in some small talk and chit chat before class started. Over time I grew quite fond of this petite student, sensing that she needed the attention and affection of a grown-up she could look up to.

One day as I was going through papers in the morning, as usual she came and sat next to me.

She said, "Mr. Graves, I don't know if I can do much writing for you today."

As I thumbed through papers I casually said, "Oh yeah. Why can't you write for me today?"

"My momma and my step-daddy whupped me and my sister with a lamp cord last night and I cain't hardly move my arm."

I stopped dead in my papers and said, "Honey, are you okay? You wanta let me see your arm?"

She was wearing a sweater and pulled up the sleeve to reveal a cross-hatching of red Xs all up and down her arm. She was a dark-skinned little girl. The fact these marks were so red and stood out against her dark coloration made it seem all the more horrible.

I spoke her name and said, "No, you don't have to write today until you get better. Tell me if anything else happens at home, okay?"

This little girl had placed an awful lot of trust in me to tell me this. But what to do? If I brought this to the attention of the authorities it might possibly make matters worse at home for her. But if I remained silent… I shuddered to think about the possibilities. I wrote a note to the vice principal, Mr. Lane, and without making a fuss of any kind that would alert the other students that something was up, I sent a trusted student to the office with my note with specific instructions that no one but Mr. Lane should get the note and that she was to give it to him and him only personally.

Later that day I caught up with Mr. Lane who told me I had done the right thing. It was mandatory to contact the authorities in the case of child abuse such as I had witnessed. And he had in fact contacted social services. I told Mr. Lane that I worried about my student feeling that I had betrayed her trust. He told me something very wise: students often tell their teachers such things because they trust the teachers to do something about it. My student missed class the next few days. When she returned I called her to my desk to sit next to me. I told her I was sorry that I may have betrayed her trust but that I was worried about her safety. And that I felt I had to do something to protect her.

She nodded her head and said, "People came to the house and talked to Momma and my step-daddy and told them not to hit us again."

And that was that. To my knowledge she was never beaten again. I often wonder what happened to her and if she would remember me at all.

Marquita is a name that will live in infamy in the halls of Hickory Ridge Middle School. Marquita was a loud, brassy, overbearing, grossly obese female student who had smart-aleck backtalk and sass for anything any of her teachers said or did in the classroom. She kept up a constant hail of unwelcome comments and retorts and any disciplinary remarks to her were an open invitation to a verbal battle. She was easily the most despised student in our teachers' group of five teachers. Our particular teachers' group all taught the same core students.

If one of us had Marquita in our class, we all had her.

Marquita lorded over the classroom like a Mafia don. The other girls were terrified of her and the boys steered clear as well because she was an aggressive sexual bully towards them. Other teachers in my group had confiscated notes Marquita passed in class—which by the way can be shockingly revealing on many levels—in which she freely offered sexual treats to boys willing to show her due respect and a little love. A lot of sexual adventuring among pre-teens is nothing more than fantasy talk, but with a few 12-year-olds with heightened knowledge and sensibilities, just about anything is possible. Seventh graders do get pregnant and a few get STDs, usually from predatory older kids and particularly step-dads and mommas' boyfriends. Marquita's personality was undoubtedly formed by being the biggest, baddest, and fattest in her class. She dared anyone to laugh at her.

As her report card went out, so did the note from our teachers' group that we would like to meet with one of Marquita's parents to discuss her behavior. A meeting was set up with her mother and there in the conference room was a woman who looked just like Marquita in thirty more years. She was big, she was fierce, and she wore a permanent frown. Marquita sat next to her mother as we began detailing the many behavior issues we were having with our student.

Marquita and her mother silently listened and as Marquita objected to a comment by one of the teachers her mom let fly with a hard backhand to Marquita's mouth telling her loudly, "Shut up! You the reason we sitting here!"

Marquita's lip spurted blood and instantly swelled to three

times its normal size. The teachers were all in shock and said nothing, just pushed a box of tissues to Marquita for her lip.

We reported this to our principal who told us that only she had the power to stop a parent from lashing out at a child and it had to be done in her presence. For this one and only time I felt sorry for Marquita and gained insight into why she was who she was. I'd be very curious to know where she is today.

Jamie was a student I very much liked. Handsome and light-skinned, he had a pleasant personality, a winning smile, and was always open to anything the least bit humorous. Then for reasons none of us teachers understood, he began acting out. He was an above-average student, one who showed up faithfully, turned in his work, and made good grades. We were concerned especially because he had shown promise, but was now taking a walk down a darker road. And so we appealed to the parents.

A meeting was set up with Jamie, Jamie's dad, me, and our new assistant principal, Mr. Stevens, who had taken the place of the much-missed Mr. Lane. Mr. Stevens was a six-foot-eight former basketball player and coach who had worked his way into administration. He also brought his wooden paddle with him which he talked our principal into using—the first corporal whacks of the school year. Jamie's parents, I learned, were divorced and Jamie rarely saw his father and they weren't on particularly good terms. It showed.

Jamie's father was one of those stereotypical black men with ostentatiously proper manners and an overly-dramatic and precise way of talking. As we told him about the problems we were having with Jamie he switched from Jekyll to Hyde in minutes. He began to shout at Jamie, daring him to respond. Jamie sat silently, biting his lip, staring forward to avoid the brewing confrontation. The father got up out of his seat, got within an inch of Jamie's face and began to taunt and berate him as the assistant principal and I sat aghast. Tears began to roll from Jamie's eyes and finally he burst out with a cry of utter anguish. The father then grabbed Jamie by the throat, toppled him out of his chair onto the floor and was choking the life out of him. I was frozen, not knowing what to do. Mr. Stevens had his wits about him, thankfully, and quickly ran over and pulled the berserk father off his son. I regained my bearings and grabbed Jamie up off the floor and hustled him down the hall and hid him in a closet until I was certain his father was out of the building.

As I walked Jamie to safety I apologized for what had happened. I told him I never would have asked to meet his dad if I knew this would happen. I told him to stay put as quietly as possible until the coast was clear. I returned to the conference room and the father sat there smiling like a mule eating briers, as if not a thing had happened. We quickly dismissed our meeting and made sure the dad was gone. Then I went and got Jamie and walked him to his next class. Jamie's behavior improved noticeably after that and in particular he was good in my class. We had silently bonded that day and from then on he knew he could trust me and that I would always look out for him.

I have spent the better part of my life in schools. I have seen many things, some of which I recount here. But I have never seen a man assault his son like that and I hope to never see it again, although there have been some close calls. Of course nothing happened to Jamie's father even though in my opinion he deserved time in jail. He could have killed his son that day, no question, and he certainly could have maimed him for life.

Over the years I have occasionally told these stories to other people, people who I know damn well had a hard time believing that such a thing could really happen. Believe me, in Memphis City Schools not only do these things happen, they happen every day.

I caught a male student up on a female student in the girls' bathroom. Girls were running screaming out of the bathroom because a boy was in there. He almost wanted to fight me when I hauled him out, not the first or last time physical violence was threatened by a student.

Every middle school teacher knew that girls were much more prone to fight than the boys. We often discussed why. My opinion was that boys take fighting much more seriously than girls who generally speaking don't get hurt much beyond some hair pulling. But boys fighting can hurt each other and no boy wants to lose a fight and his dignity right along with it. So they avoid fighting unless the grievance is just too heavy.

One of my favorite people at Hickory Ridge was a veteran guidance counselor, an older African-American lady I will call Mrs. Fanning, who knew all, saw all, and whose quips were as funny as any television comedian's. The principal required us to stay on campus during lunch period to monitor the lunchroom. From time immemorial, teachers have sat at their own table in the cafeterias of this country, keeping an eye on the students.

I'll never forget Mrs. Fanning pointing out one of our few white kids at Hickory Ridge and telling me, "See that little white boy? Notice how he always sits right in front of that big support column? I mean every day. Every single day. Know why he does that? So he can see anything that's coming at him. So nobody can come up from behind and do something to him."

And, of course, Mrs. Fanning was right.

There were times when we could smell a fight in the air. Teachers develop a sixth sense for such things and even though the cafeteria looked normal and on the surface everything seemed as usual you could *feel* something brewing. One lunch period the fight vibe was undeniable. At the teachers' table that day we *all* felt it.

Mrs. Fanning in her most cynical guise said, "I ain't breaking up no fight today."

Others chimed in that they too were standing down for any such shenanigans. Not five minutes later two girls sitting at the same lunch table got up and began to scream at each other, the familiar prelude to physical conflict. Boys would bump chests before throwing punches. Nobody at the teachers' table got up, including me. Next thing we knew the girls were grabbing each others' hair and pulling it out by the handful. Then they were windmilling their arms at each other, the girl version of throwing punches. We sat and watched.

Finally, when the girls were nearly at the stage of removing their shoes and socks—the mark of a real throwdown—

the coach (an excitable young white guy who by benching misbehaving students could keep our athletes pretty much in line) and I went over to the girls, got between them, fists flying, and broke them apart as they each kept a handful of the other's hair.

One pretty and demure little transfer student came into our classes mid-semester who had a serious record of expulsion from other schools. We didn't quite get it because she was so soft spoken and well-mannered. She never caused any trouble whatsoever. Then one day one of the boy basketball players, as boys will do, was yah-yahing at this girl and made the mistake of under his breath calling her "cornbread," which in African-American circles in Memphis is a deep insult, meaning you are nothing but a country bumpkin, or as one of my black girlfriends used to say a country bunker. This petite girl whipped off her leather belt and began to flay the basketball player with it, knocking him to the floor, him trying his best to protect his face with his hands.

She stopped to take off her mini-boots and I thought to myself, "Uh-oh, now it's on."

I couldn't get near the girl because she was slinging her belt like Bruce Lee with his nunchucks. Instead, I got the basketball player up and out of the room and the girl picked up my wastebasket and threw it out in the hall, where all the clang and clatter instantly alerted the other teachers who came running.

I took the basketball player to the office and pleaded with the assistant principal to go easy on him: he hadn't raised a hand to this girl in spite of the fists of fury. The girl?

Transferred to yet another school. We determined amongst ourselves that the girl had serious mental issues. And she was dangerous. At 12 years old.

In the middle of the second semester I was called into the principal's office for a conference. The following is what transpired:

Principal: Mr. Graves, I've heard from several mothers that you called one of our students a "jackass."

Me: Actually, what I said was "You need to stop that jackass laugh of yours."

Principal: Mr. Graves, you can't use a word like that around these students.

Me: I'm confused. That boy looks and sounds just like a jackass when he laughs. It's ridiculous.

Principal: But they don't know what that word means. They think, and these mothers think, you are using profanity.

Me: What? Jackass? It means a donkey. It's *not* profanity.

Principal: I know that, and you know that, but *they* don't know that.

Me: My God! Jackass is a term used in the King James Bible, for God's sake.

Principal: And that's why we have separation of church and state Mr. Graves.

She was using what we teachers called "principal's logic."

Gorilla Pimp

BY THE END OF the school year there was no name I had not been called by the students at one time or another. Typically the offending word would be said under their breath but loud enough for me to hear and for the other students to hear as well. I was called an asshole frequently, son of a bitch, *puta* (which they had picked up from the Hispanic students), dick, dickhead, prick, fucker, motherfucker, whitey, honky, dog, dawg, niggah, and most surprisingly, nigger.

I was flat out called a nigger several times. My most common reply to such words was, "I guess you think you are hurting my feelings by saying that don't you? Do I look hurt?"

When they saw that I hadn't flinched generally they, and I, would move past it. The only time I would take action is when a "fuck you" was directed at me. That I wouldn't put up with. That is where I drew the line.

Sometime around mid-year, I heard students saying "gorilla pimp" and laughing while doing an eyeslide in my direction. I caught on pretty quick that they were calling me that, gorilla pimp, and that this nickname would probably stick. It did. No student ever called me that to my face, mind you, but I heard it a lot circulating in the back of the classroom. I learned this was a popular rap song by a scowling Memphis-based rapper named Project Pat who was related to Juicy J of Three Six Mafia, the biggest Memphis rap act of that decade. The lyrics are about the last thing 7th graders need to be hearing, full of violence, mayhem, misogyny, and throat cutting. A sample of the lyrics is: *"I'mma go-rilla pimp you can call me great ape/Knockin' teefus out ya mouth need to get ya shit straight."* I don't think Bob Dylan has much to worry about.

One class a girl was on a rant about some white people who had behaved rudely to her somewhere.

"I hate white people," she said looking straight at me.

The other students quickly murmured and glanced at me to see how I would react.

"Sorry you feel that way," is all I said.

The next day the same girl came up to me and apologized.

"I don't hate all white people," she said.

"I'm glad to hear it," I said, smiling.

Any time I would ever give it back, say the wrong thing, there would be repercussions. The day of the 9/11 attack on the World Trade Center one of the nicest and smartest boys in all my classes had been home part of the day and had seen the first news of an aircraft flying into one of the World Trade Center buildings. He came up to me in the early afternoon as I recall and asked if I knew what had happened. None of the teachers had yet gotten word of the event and the way the student told it to me I thought a small airplane, a single-engine Piper Cub-type aircraft had accidentally flown into one of the buildings. Later that day, of course, we learned of the full incident.

The next day the students were full of questions about 9/11. Many of them had seen videos of people leaping to their deaths from the burning buildings and were deeply disturbed by what they had seen. They couldn't make sense of it.

"Mr. Graves, why were those people jumping out of those buildings to die?" several asked me.

"Have you ever really burned yourself," I asked.

Many nodded.

"Then imagine heat and fire burning you up. Would you stay in that heat or jump? It's a terrible choice, right?"

Later that day a group of boys, including the honor student who had first told me about something happening at the World Trade Center, was laughing about the attack. Laughing about those people leaping to their deaths. Us teachers were plenty shaken by the 9/11 events. Hearing those boys laughing about death and destruction, the worst such incident in American history, enraged me. In my time as a student it was unthinkable to make light of such an event where innocent American blood was shed.

I scolded the boys and under my breath said, "Idiots."

They heard me.

A couple of weeks later the vice principal came to me and said "one of your students' fathers is here to see you." I was on my one-hour break and instructed that he should come up to my room. The student was this honor roll student and when I saw him I instantly knew what was in store. It was because I called him and the others an idiot. The father was a deputy sheriff in uniform with his sidearm in full view. And he did not look the least bit happy.

I have never sweated a parent-teacher conference as much as this one. The father wearing his uniform, with a .38 pistol at his side, was fully meant to intimidate me and put fear into my heart. And it sure worked. I was literally trembling. I apologized. I tried to explain myself. I told the father how upset I was about 9/11 and how the students laughing simply got to me.

"Something like this can affect a boy for life," the father said to me, steel in his eyes.

I've managed to talk my way out of a lot of things in my life and talked my way in to just as many. Somehow I babbled my way through this one and the father finally seemed satisfied that he had rubbed enough of a scare into me and left. This incident still haunts me. If only I had held back and kept my cool with those boys.

At the same time, I feel now and felt then those boys deserved being told they were idiots. It makes my teeth grind just thinking of how they haw-hawed about people jumping to their deaths. I have no understanding of how these young people could be so immune to the lives and feelings of others. And someone needed to set them straight.

A day or two after 9/11 the principal had told the school over the intercom that at noon that day the school would observe a minute of silence in honor of those who had died during 9/11. As the clock struck noon I was in the cafeteria eating my lunch and no other teacher was in view in the lunchroom. At noon no one came over the loudspeaker to begin the minute of silence. I am not a praying man, and I'm not one of those who wraps myself in the flag either. But I felt

I had to do something, so I called for the attention of every student in the lunchroom, asked them to stand, and told them we would observe our minute of silence. It went well except for a few of the older 8th grade boys who were cutting up. I gave them a hard look but for once didn't say anything. And this is how we observed 9/11 that day. Had it not been for me, those students would not have observed 9/11 at all.

Bad Behavior

BAD BEHAVIOR CAN CATCH fire in the classroom. One back-talking student can easily lead to two then three and things can get out of hand instantly if discipline isn't quick and consistent. In one afternoon class I corrected a girl student for acting up. She began to shout back at me, and like an electric current traveling point-to-point, one girl after another stood up at her desk, waving and pointing at me, screaming and out of control. There was no shouting them down; I simply bit my tongue and waited until they had exhausted themselves. I asked my neighboring teacher across the hall to watch my class for a few minutes and marched the girls straight to the principal's office.

I was seething inside but aloof enough around the principal's office to retain full composure. The principal wasn't in, but the new assistant principal was and I explained what had happened.

I told him, "The principal keeps turning these kids around and sending them right back to me without any punishment or discipline. That won't do. I want action on this. These students went too far and I must maintain some order in my classroom. I'd like to meet with their parents and I want some discipline to happen. If it doesn't, I may have to make some calls to the Board."

That last statement was a threat and I meant every word. I knew I didn't want another year in middle school hell and that it wouldn't derail my career one bit by reporting lax discipline at Hickory Ridge Middle School. The principal and staff all knew I was there by administrative appointment and that I had high-up connections at the Board. They also knew I wasn't afraid to use the juice I had.

And so the meeting was scheduled. A group of about eight angry parents, all African-American, glared at me, the lone white guy in the room, with all six of the offending girls plus our vice principal. Many of these parents had to leave their jobs to attend this meeting which factored into their anger. A white man—a big, tall white man—correcting 12-year-old African-American girls is a dicey situation at best. I knew I was in for a very rough ride but I had brought my spurs and saddle. I was ready.

Naturally, the girls had denied to their parents they had done anything wrong. Death rays shot out of the parents' eyes. As the meeting began, one parent then another began telling the others how awful a teacher I was and how I had done this thing and that thing.

Before the third parent got into her attack, I held up my hand and said loudly, "Enough! We are not here to talk about me today. We can come back for that another day if you want. But today we are going to talk about what these girls did. If you are looking to hang *me*, I'm walking out."

I meant it and the vice principal knew I meant it.

"We don't want that Mr. Graves," he said calmly. "We will keep the subject on what happened with these girls. Let's start with the girls and hear what they have to say."

The first girl began by saying "We did'n' do nothing. Mr. Graves just started yelling at us and calling us names…"

She had barely gotten those words out of her mouth when one of the other girls broke down and began to sob.

"Mr. Graves, I am so sorry we treated you that way. We was wrong. We shouldn't of been hollering at you like that and saying those things to you."

For several long seconds all you could hear was the air conditioning gently humming through the vents. One by one, in that same electrical circuit, they broke down and confessed in front of their very surprised parents. I knew then to keep my mouth shut and let the scene play out. The students apologized through a vale of tears, the parents apologized, and the vice principal apologized. I blew the smoke off the tip of my six-shooter, reholstered it, and rode off into the sunset, another day done.

Final Memories

A FEW FINAL MEMORIES of my fated year at Hickory Ridge Middle School. The cafeteria was a mandatory part of teachers' daily grind through the school day. We weren't allowed to go off campus to pick up fast food nor were we allowed to go to our cars and eat our lunch. We were stuck in the cafeteria every day of the school week with about 100 misbehaving students, half of whom were on a sugar high and just buzzing to create some mischief. The floors were littered with food refuse, particularly crumbles of chips and other greasy snacks. Flamin' Hot Cheetos were a particular favorite and there wasn't a room in the building without evidence of them, and I'd be curious as to the doctor visits incurred due to ulcerated stomachs from the over-spiced contents of those little packages.

Teachers were allowed to break in front of the long lines of students in the cafeteria to get our food first so we could sit and "monitor" students, which every single one of us hated. The cafeteria workers were all young black women and they all liked me because I always had a joke or funny greeting for them. One of the workers named Kayla was a very pretty and petite thirty-something who had a dynamite figure in her tiny little package. She had one of those high, tight superbly rounded bottoms that make for the subject of hundreds of rap songs not to mention the masturbatory fantasies of men the world over. I couldn't help but notice she always had a big smile waiting for me and would pile huge portions on my plate, much more than she should have.

Naturally I flirted and she seemed to eat it up. Even the students began to notice our carryings-on and would tease me about it. As our repartee developed we wound up swapping phone numbers and agreed to get together sometime. At some point early on in the school's second semester I called her and we wound up talking engagingly for a very long time. I knew she was single, of course, but I didn't know that at the age of 32 she had six (!!!) kids. Even after more than an hour's conversation I didn't know how many daddies were involved in this menagerie. We had agreed that we would go out for drinks but the fact of her having six children—which I knew she could not support on the salary of a cafeteria worker— gave me second and even third thoughts.

Early in March that school year Memphis had one of those late freak snows that always takes the city unprepared but shouldn't because of how frequently March gets these surprise snowstorms. The snow caused the school to be closed for the day, which didn't exactly thrill me because that meant the final day of the school year would be extended by a day. Kayla called me and asked if I would like to have those drinks we had talked about. The snow was melting and I had a four-wheel drive SUV that could handle snow and ice easily so I agreed to meet. Then I found out Kayla, who had six kids, did not have a car! I'd have to pick her up. I didn't give it much thought that this would be my first official date with a black woman.

Kayla lived very close to Hickory Ridge Middle School, within walking distance, and I drove from my Midtown home to pick her up. I was invited inside her cozy duplex where kids were busily entertaining themselves doing the things kids do. The oldest kids were in their early teens and when I did the math I figured the oldest must have been born when Kayla was around 16 years old. A daughter about the age of 12 followed her mother all through the duplex as she got ready for our "date" and this quiet, nerdy-looking little girl with big cat's eye glasses and a prim school dress seemed the complete opposite of her firecracker petite mom. The kids didn't pay any mind to the fact I happened to be white.

There was a well-known bar close by we had decided upon for drinks but she asked me to swing by a Blockbuster video store where she picked up at least 10 videotapes for her family to watch later. I was impressed with the large screen— bigger than mine—television set she had in her home that at that time had to have cost a lot more than her paycheck. Where was this money coming from?

As we settled down to drinks our conversation was warm and convivial on this chilling day. Ever the journalist, I gently probed about her life to see just who this curious and comely young woman was.

As she took a sip of her drink she asked me casually, "Do you ever go to gentlemen's clubs?"

Well, this took me aback.

"Do you mean 'gentlemen's clubs,' as in strip clubs and so forth?"

"Yeah, like that."

"Um, not really. I've been to a few in my life, of course, but they've never really been my thing. I don't like the idea of look-but-don't-touch in those places. I prefer to have my own special woman."

"I dance sometimes," she said with a sexy smile.

I'm sure I stuttered some sort of answer to this.

She went on to tell me that she fairly routinely would take a bus to Nashville and would dance at some of the better paying strip clubs there. She danced in Nashville so that no one in Memphis would know she was a stripper. She pledged me to secrecy about this other life she led. Her "act" was to dress as a Catholic schoolgirl in a uniform that she would then slowly peel off as she gyrated to whatever music she had chosen. Because she was so petite and little girl-looking, she claimed she was a big hit at the clubs and came home from a weekend of dancing with a whole lot more money than she made in the cafeteria. So, that was how she could afford a two-thousand dollar television set.

I well knew what went on in those gentlemen's clubs and the thought of Kayla performing lap dances with sweaty men and providing sexual favors in the back shadows of those clubs pretty much ended things for me on the spot. We drank and ate appetizers and carried on with good-natured conversation but I really could not wait to drop her at her house and let that one sink into the swamp of my past.

We saw each other at school as usual and I kept up a

pretense of being interested, but I wasn't. I never called her again. Only a few weeks after the end of the school year, when I was doing my level best to wash Hickory Ridge Middle School right out of my head, I received a call late one night. It was Kayla. She was crying, literally, about needing money. She asked if she could "borrow" forty dollars until her next paycheck. She was desperate.

My dad was tight with money. He hated to be told that because he felt he was simply being sensible, and he knew how hard he'd had to work all his life to manage to save anything. I didn't fall far from that tree. Life is hard, money is tough, and half the planet is plotting to take it away. I've never been a spender, I've never been a borrower, and I certainly haven't been a lender, which means I have less friends than some of you.

I did a quick calculation and decided it was smarter money to give her forty bucks and see her gone forever—because I knew damn well I'd never see a penny of the loan again—than politely decline which would still give her an opening to contact me further down the line if she got hard up for money again. I gambled that once I gave her the money she'd never call again because I would always have the argument that she never paid back any of that first loan.

So, I agreed to "loan" her forty dollars. We rendezvoused near the Board of Education building and it was a fellow cafeteria worker I recognized who had to haul her across town since Kayla had no car. She hugged me and kissed me for loaning her the money and waved as she left the parking lot. I never heard from her again.

I confess. I'm curious about where she is and what she's

doing now. If only I could remember her last name.

*   *   *

Passing the restrooms on the way to the cafeteria one day boys were bouncing out of the boys' restroom hollering, yelling, carrying on. There was obviously a commotion going on in the restroom, so I went in to investigate. One of my male students, one of those who still looked like a little boy, was holding his stomach and throwing up all over the restroom. Thus the boys running out of the restroom and jumping everywhere to get away from the flying vomit.The sick boy was horror-struck. He didn't know, literally, what was happening to him. It was obvious to me that the kid did not know how to throw up. I caught him by the arm and pulled him over to a toilet.

"Here son," I said. "If you need to throw up lean over the toilet bowl and throw up in there."

He nodded okay and leaned over the bowl, letting out a noisy spume of vomit. I couldn't stand much of this, so I patted him on the back and said, "Go see the nurse when you feel okay enough to go to her."

Which he did. The next day he was much improved. When I quizzed him about what had happened he admitted that he had been eating candy all morning (remember that the principal allowed this) and then ate a big lunch on top of that. It was too much for his stomach and so he became nauseated and threw up, the first time in his life that he could remember. He admitted he didn't know what was going on.

And some people think teachers have it easy.

Break on Through
(To the Other Side)

OFF AND ON THROUGHOUT my adult life I have gone
to sales—estate sales, yard sales, rummage sales, church sales,
you name it. I love the idea of stumbling across something of
value that goes unrecognized by others. Two styles of furniture
and home decorations particularly interest me: art deco
and Mid-Century Modernist. Plus, I simply like interesting
collectibles. My 100-year-old Midtown home in Memphis is
decorated (cluttered) with many of my better finds from such
sales.

I also collect vinyl record albums. I saw in the paper one
Saturday morning circa 2001 that a particular estate sale listed
a large collection of LPs for sale, so I made plans to go check
it out. I have learned not to get in a hurry at sales; impatience
will cause you to overlook something you may regret skipping
over. So, I entered the house and began leisurely scanning the
goods, noting what was interesting and what was the usual
flotsam found at every such sale.

As I entered the kitchen, one of the estate sale workers
was seated at a small folding table, there to help price the

merchandise. I looked at her; she looked at me. Then she stood up to greet me and when she did it was like in one of those movies where there is an establishing shot of a person in full frame and the camera rapidly zooms up to the face in extreme close-up. I could swear that a shaft of light from on high shone through a window haloing her head. Perhaps the angels sang as well.

She was an African-American. She wore a classic black skirt with black hosiery, and her hair was pulled back into a neat bun. She had an almost perfect, trim figure. When she smiled her teeth were like 100-watt lightbulbs. Her Bambi eyelashes all seemed to be gesturing "come my dear." My pulse tripled. No fool I, of course, chatted her up. When I ran out of idle conversation and didn't want to appear too anxious, I asked where the record albums were. She walked me to them. I flipped through the records quickly and found only the bane of record collecting, classical music and easy listening dreck. I took one to buy just to pretend some sort of interest and she walked me to the check-out spot. She seemed just as interested in me as I was in her. She waved good-bye.

The entire next week I planned my next move, hoping the estate sale company would be having another sale scheduled for the following weekend. Hallelujah, they did! Putting on my coolest casual clothes, I went to the sale, which was at a different location, and there she was. She instantly spotted me and with a smile we chatted and as I recall she asked me to walk with her out to her car; she needed to fetch something for the day ahead of her and it was a way to talk for a bit before she had to return to her job. I wasted no time. I got her phone number and her name (we'll call her Lisa) and we made a date.

The following weekend we agreed to meet at a popular nightspot on Beale Street, Memphis' famous tourist attraction and once-notorious party district for blacks. Lisa was dressed smartly in form-fitting jeans but was so nervous throughout the evening that it was difficult gauging exactly how interested in me she was and if our relationship would go any further than this one date.

As we were parting later than evening I said to her with a big grin, "So do you believe in goodnight kisses on the first date?"

"No!" she replied firmly.

I thought this would be the end of things between us but she surprised me by inviting me to a party at her boss's ornate Midtown home the very next evening. She told me she would be bartending for the event but that I'd be welcome to hang with her and enjoy the party.

"My boss, by the way, is very gay," she told me, "and most of the guests are going to be gay, too."

That didn't phase me one way or the other and as long as I'd be with her I figured all would be well. The next evening Lisa was dressed in a man's tuxedo and was like some glamourpuss from a 1930s Hollywood comedy. While she worked I mixed and mingled among the crowd and was instantly seized upon as somebody new to the gang. Numerous well-dressed men graciously introduced themselves to me, firing questions to see who and what I was. I could see the disappointment in their eyes when I explained that I was there with Lisa. Lisa was very amused watching the boys hit on me all evening.

As things began to wrap up at the party a younger fellow with longish hair and a porn-stache started hovering around me. An even younger man who was conspicuously his partner saw me being chatted up and sidled over to quash it. They began to bicker right in front of me and the younger man huffed that he was leaving and slammed the door behind him.

"Oh well," said the partner, "I hope he doesn't cry."

And then he laughed, letting me know that it was *me* he had his sights on. In a few minutes he began to talk about how horny he was. To the point, this one.

All this took place right in front of Lisa who was grinning from ear to ear at my discomfort. I finally made it clear that I was there with Lisa that night and with many promises to stay in touch, my new gay friend finally left. Lisa and I laughed about this our whole relationship.

As we parted that night I asked Lisa, "So, do you kiss on the *second* date?"

"No!" she shot back just as seriously as the night before.

As she prepared to drive away she winked and said, "Call me."

It was our third date and I hoped something would happen. Somewhere around the middle of the night, however, things took an unusual turn and Lisa began to reveal some painful and disturbing parts of her troubled life. A constant in my life is that people tell me things. Secret things. Things they don't tell other people. There is something in me that people simply trust and many, many times I've had people unburden themselves with me lending an attentive and supportive ear. This night was no different with the exception that somehow we had unburdened ourselves of all but our underclothes and were lying wrapped in one another's arms on my bed.

Even then I realized this was some sort of test. If I could be skin-to-skin with Lisa and not pounce or make an idiot of myself begging for sex then I could be regarded as safe. Oddly for me, I was caught up in the moment and denied myself the sexual feelings that I knew might spoil this otherwise intense and intimate evening. Once this trust issue had been resolved, Lisa became the most gifted and ferocious lover I ever had. No white girl in my life came close to the erotic spell she cast over me. All my friends noticed how captivated I was.

I had been under the impression up until this point, that black people's skin felt different from white people's. I thought it had a slightly more leathery feel and I would have bet money that I could have told a white person from a black person by touching their skin. There was nothing but pure soft and supple with Lisa however. She felt wonderful and velvety smooth. Like virtually every black woman I've known, she slathered herself in skin cream to keep her skin nice and soft and to avoid the "ashiness" that is so frowned upon in the culture. Lisa felt no different from any white women I had been with. So she dispelled that bit of humbug for me.

Lisa wasn't open to everything on the sexual palette. But what she was agreeable to more than made up for what she wasn't. She took more pure delight in sex than any woman I had previously been with and because she was so fit and flexible she introduced me to things I hadn't thought possible. She always teased me that she had to "teach" me how to be a sex partner up to her standards. I hate to admit it, but she may have been right.

Thus began one of the most intense and tumultuous years of my life. Lisa to me was one of the most beautiful creatures I had ever laid eyes on. She was a competitive body builder, and I discovered that there were two types of females involved in the sport. One type wanted to gain muscle mass and distort themselves physically, much as male bodybuilders do. The other type is after an Olympic ideal where muscles are defined, in proportion, and beautiful aesthetically. Lisa was firmly in the latter camp and did not want to look freakish in any way. Exactly why she was attracted to me, I will never know because I am a long, long way from an Olympic ideal. Holding this embodiment of perfection naked in my arms is one of the great thrills of my life.

Lisa had been married and divorced twice (actually three times, I found out later) and lived on her own with her meek and pretty teen-aged daughter. Lisa was from a notoriously rough Memphis neighborhood, Orange Mound, and her backstory was filled with violence, murder, roaches, rats, and the kinds of things a nice white boy like me knew nothing about. She admitted to me that she could barely read and her mangling of the English language would have been comical had it not been so sad. She lived in a small but well-tended home in an equally rough Memphis ghetto, Binghampton. Lisa struggled with a succession of jobs in addition to her estate sale work to keep this particular roof over her head and I always felt bad that she never seemed to find firm footing.

We were opposites in every way: I was a writer and aca-demic; she never held a book in her hands. I was interested in intellectual pursuits. She was interested in Tyler Perry's *Madea* movies. I was not religious. She was not only religious, she firmly believed in the spirit world and claimed she had special sight and powers. With the exception of the *Madea* flicks, she didn't like movies. I never missed a single weekend at the cinema. I was a rock and roller; she listened to R&B. For an entire year we did not miss a single day seeing each other. This kind of intensity leads to high drama, and some of our fights were epic. Lisa was expert at playing head games and manipulation. It seemed as if there was not a single moment I wasn't stressed about one problem or another in our relationship.

When I nonchalantly mentioned to my mother that I had gone on my first date with Lisa, a black woman, the blow-back was instantaneous and furious. To my Mom I had crossed a line that had been painted in big, yellow do-not-cross double stripes for over a century. I tried to downplay the whole thing, but a day later there was a very long message on my answer machine. Mom told me that dating a black woman was the "worst thing you have ever done to me." She told me I was not raised to ever do any such thing, that I knew better, how dare I, didn't I know how this hurt her, and how low class I was stooping to go with a black woman. In my adult life I had never had such an ass-chewing from my Mom. My father had passed away in 1980. Lord only knows what he would have done had he been alive.

I loved my mother very much and always did my best to respect her. I did not think she would react so violently to me being with a black woman. But I was wrong. So a day later after a lot of thinking about what she said I called her, told her I had listened to everything in the message she left, appreciated her concern, loved her very much, but that it needed to be my decision about who I dated. She was upset and disappointed, but we hung in there together. We were, after all, family.

About a year into the relationship with Lisa, she announced that the relationship had gotten too "heavy" and that she would be moving to Florida. She claimed that after this particular night, she wouldn't be seeing me any longer and would not be in contact with me in the future. That was it. It was over.

This took me quite by surprise, and for one of the few times in my life I was plunged into a very serious depression that worried me and everyone who was close to me. After this I fully understood the term "walking the black dog." The depression hit me like the flu—the real flu, not a "touch" of the flu that people claim they get. The real flu has you sick as a dog on your back for a week, all but unable to move. My depression was much like that. I could only sleep for two hours at a time. Once awake, I would be drowsy again within a couple of hours. This terrible cycle went on for a week. My friends and family grew worried that I might be suicidal. I wasn't, but I was certainly mentally sick. I had experienced a few moments of depression at odd times in my life, but nothing like this. Although I am positive Lisa's ultimatum is what triggered this depression, I cannot help but wonder if some chemical change in my brain brought on the full-scale black dog. After a week, I slowly began to recover and by the time I heard again from Lisa I was close to my normal self.

Although I was told she would be moving to Florida and

never speaking to me again, of course, that didn't happen. She never left Memphis and she wanted to resume our relationship. Reluctantly, I started seeing her again, but the thrill was gone. I also found out during this waiting period that she had been toying with the idea of reuniting with her second—no, third—husband. I was totally soured on the whole thing, but stayed with it for the occasional fringe benefit. I also began dating others on the sly and making myself unavailable most weekends. The end was near and the buzzards were doing figure eights.

During my relationship with Lisa I was exposed to my first violence in a relationship. We had terrible rows during our time together and there was lots of shouting, shrieking, and phones that went dead in the middle of an argument. Once, right in the middle of the throes of love Lisa reached up to give me a playful love bite on my bicep. It felt like a wolverine had taken a plug out of me, ruining the moment in a split second. In the days to follow the bite mark became a very large yellow and purplish bruise that I mostly covered up with my shirts. One warm day when I wasn't going to work I slipped on a polo shirt to do odds and ends around the house.

My next-door neighbor, Doug Lowrie, who was a retired Memphis policeman, came over to chat and when I stretched to reach for something he saw the ugly mark on my arm.

"What the hell happened to you?" he queried with a frown.

"Ah, Lisa bit me right in the middle of getting it on," I replied. "Hurt like a motherfucker, too."

"What did she do that for?"

"She said she meant it as just a love bite, but it sure didn't feel like one."

"Damn! You know, don't you, that she could be arrested for doing that? Man, that's abuse. That's no love bite. I can't stand that woman. I don't know how you put up with her."

He wasn't the only one who didn't like Lisa.

One day Lisa and I were mildly bickering about some minor thing when out of nowhere she punched me in the jaw. Just like that, boom, with her balled up fist. It didn't really hurt and it didn't cause any damage but the level of shock was off the scale. I told her she needed to leave and go home, and after trying to say she was sorry with no response from me, she quietly left. I sometimes think I'm much too forgiving and the relationship carried on. A few months later, again in a low-key disagreement over something, she slapped me. That was the last of many final straws. Our days together were numbered.

Before we leave Lisa, I want to tell one last tale. I am pretty much a skeptic when it comes to anything metaphysical, so I did not for a moment believe in Lisa's ghosts and spirit world. She told some great stories, that I will say, but nothing that I believed in.

One week during our relationship Lisa was house-sitting for her boss who owned the estate sale company. He was a nice if rather flamboyant gay man who lived in a small mansion (is that an oxymoron?) in a chic and swanky neighborhood in Memphis. The house was stocked with a museum's worth of pricey antiques. But I'm kind of like the actor Billy Bob Thornton. Ornate antiques make me a little sick.

Lisa invited me to spend the night with her in this

mahvelous house. Like Gore Vidal, I don't believe in turning down television appearances or sex. So off I went. When the evening was done and our passions spent, we prepared for sleep. I saw that we would be sleeping in an antique sled bed, not my favorite accommodation exactly, but it would do. As I slept I began to have some of the scariest dreams in memory. I can visualize them to this day. Against a black darkness, evil ugly faces like Halloween horror masks would lurch at me threateningly, screaming and shouting vile words. It was utterly terrifying. And then I awoke abruptly. Staring at me with her face only inches away was Lisa, her eyes wide open and peering straight into mine.

She said, "Don't worry Tom, I saw them, too. I told them to go away and leave you alone. They won't bother you anymore so you can go back to sleep."

I then drifted off into a most wonderful, restful sleep.

The next morning when I woke up I remembered the whole thing. As Lisa fixed breakfast I excitedly probed her about what had happened.

"I told you I had powers and could see things, but you wouldn't believe me. I saw those evil spirits in your dreams. They wanted you to leave this house and be gone from here, but I told them to go away and leave you alone and they did. You were a stranger to them and they didn't like you and they wanted you to go."

Well, this astounded me, and still does. I see Lisa from time to time and I am lucky in that I am still very good friends with most of my exes. When I bring this bizarre episode up, she is always nonchalant, as if it's no big deal. Considering that

I've never experienced anything remotely like it, to me, it is a very big deal.

Two years into our relationship and Lisa and I were barely seeing each other. In the meantime, two things had happened: I had gotten a free offer to join a new dating site called Match. com. I had also thought about leaving the United States for a while on a Fulbright Award to teach in Senegal in West Africa. I wanted to research the African roots of American blues music along the Senegambian coast. Coincidentally, I had seen an interesting ad for a writer to write legal briefs in laymen's language in Sierra Leone that related to war crimes trials there. So I applied for the Fulbright in Senegal and the writing job in Sierra Leone. And I joined Match.com hoping to catch the eye of someone in Memphis.

I had no idea these three things would thread together in a most unexpected way.

My Heart Takes You

AS MY RELATIONSHIP WITH Lisa was slowly circling the drain, I was discovering the travails of online dating through this new thing called Match.com. Someone at Match.com had a stroke of genius in the marketing of this innovative and defining computer dating service by offering a long free trial, enough to get just about any single person hooked. So many faces, so many flavors, so many flaws. At least that was my initial experience. There were the ultra-religious, the vegetarians, the pet-besotted, the Tea Partiers, the rabid Ole Miss fans, the ones who just loved to read—John Grisham, Stephen King, Danielle Steel. The middle-aged ones who dressed like *Girls Gone Wild* on spring break, the cleavage practically dancing in your face. The many who had no formal education, which was in ample evidence in their spelling-challenged self-descriptions.

Still, I managed a few awkward dates, and one well-educated and refined African-American I managed to date more than once. Several dates later she called me and nervously confessed that she was having second thoughts about dating a white man. My take on it was that her large family from deep down in Mississippi would have a hard time with it, not her.

I took the rejection on the chin and we agreed to be friends, which usually means that's the end of things. But, indeed, we did become good friends and remain so.

About the time I was going to let my trial offer to Match. com expire, I discovered by a faulty click that a member could seek prospective matches from all over the world, not just the U.S. I had no real thought of dating someone from overseas —that seemed like a dead end; just think of the logistics involved. But it was fun to see pictures of women from, say, Iceland or Argentina, and read their descriptions, which often proved quite interesting. Because I had applied for a Fulbright teaching award in Senegal and the writing job in Sierra Leone, I checked to see if there were any Match.com members there. As I recall, I found two. One, named Asha Kalu, was from Sierra Leone and currently living in Dakar, Senegal. Seeing as how this covered two bases, I messaged her and asked about these countries and told her of my job applications there. The picture of Asha was of a thin, pretty, rather sad-looking West African with lovely almond-shaped eyes, which I would learn is a common feature of the Senegalese.

She quickly responded in a friendly fashion and explained that Senegal was a wonderful and stable country with much to offer and that Sierra Leone, where she was born, was still recovering from several years of brutal civil war, whose horrors were coming to light in the war crimes trials that related to the job offer I had applied for. She explained that the United Nations had relocated her from Sierra Leone as a refugee to Senegal, the latter of which had been her father's home country.

She asked me about myself, and I had yet more questions about Senegal and Sierra Leone. What started as a question-and-answer session between us rapidly evolved into an ongoing dialogue. Neither of us mentioned romance, and as there was a 16-year gap in our ages I felt she was too young for me. Dakar is five hours ahead of Memphis time. If I emailed her at night and went off to work teaching the next day, by the time I returned home a nice email from Senegal would typically be waiting for me. I was only sporadically seeing Lisa at this point; there were long gaps where we didn't communicate. Having a daily email from someone halfway around the world who seemed genuinely interested in me could not have come at a more opportune time. I almost felt as if I were developing a crush on this Asha, truth be told, as impossible as such a thing would ever be.

I soon learned that Asha was not her real name. Asha was her adopted baptismal name at the Assembly of God church where she was a new parishioner who had converted from Islam. She also sang in the church choir and was a soloist as well. She claimed people thought she had an angelic voice. Her real name was Fatima Magoro. She had been married to a man named Alimamy Sesay in Sierra Leone, who she claimed had been a major in the Sierra Leone army. He had retired from service and was working in the family business of building fishing boats. They lived in an upper-class section of Freetown, Sierra Leone, and one night rebel forces broached a U.N. barricade where they went house-to-house on a rampage, robbing, raping, and pillaging. The rebels broke into the Sesays' home in the dead of the night and demanded that

Alimamy Sesay—the former army major—join them. He refused. They aimed their rifles and Fatima hysterically stood her ground in front of her husband to protect him. One of the rebels clubbed her in the head with the butt of his rifle, knocking her cold and opening an ugly wound on her forehead.

As she told the story, she woke up in an army hospital where neighbors had taken her. When she came to her full senses the doctors informed her that her husband had been taken into the street and shot dead. They also told her that she was pregnant, something she and her husband had tried to achieve without success over the six years of their marriage. Alimamy Sesay was exactly my age, 16 years older than Fatima. This made my developing interest in her not quite so ludicrous, or at least so I told myself. I should stop right here and say that at one point Fatima had told me her husband knew of her pregnancy and was delighted they were expecting a child. Later she denied ever having told me that; she insisted she learned she was pregnant in the hospital. She also told me that she called her husband "Major" in deference to his high position in the military. Later she told me she only called him by his first name, "Alimamy," and denied she had told me she called him "Major."

Because she had military connections, she was taken to the United Nations there in Sierra Leone and declared herself a refugee. Within days she was flown to Dakar, Senegal and permanently relocated there. Many things about her story checked out under scrutiny. When we met I could see the jagged scar right at her hairline from being hit by a rifle butt. Over the years as I heard these stories the facts as she related them were mostly consistent. However, as with her pregnancy, I occasionally got more than one version of certain events. There was an awful lot of fuzz in her backstory.

For example, it was unclear how she earned money during the early part of her life in Senegal. She claimed she was placed with different families, some of which barely fed her. She says she eventually received a refugee stipend from the United Nations, which she could live on, and eventually got a beautician's license from a school that the United Nations paid for. She worked in a beauty shop owned by a white Frenchwoman. She had records of her schooling, so there were no doubts there. Fatima was never one to do without. How she lived in the style she was accustomed to is something I may never know.

She had given birth to a daughter, Adama, during her first years in Senegal. Fatima talked a good deal about raising her daughter and also the son of a male friend named Abdul who I would hear more about in the coming weeks and months. How she juggled childcare with beauty school and later working in a beauty salon I do not know.

I can type a thousand-word email in 30 minutes. As I was drawn into a deeper online relationship with Fatima, my emails got longer and longer and hers nearly matched mine in length. I learned that she would go every day to a cyber café in Dakar, rent a computer, and write me. By this time I was well-used to the photograph of her on Match.com. Then I discovered that she had a second photo posted there. When I clicked on this picture that had so far eluded me I was stunned. There she was, nearly six-feet tall, long, leggy, and of an exotic beauty that took my breath away. She was smiling and her teeth were dentally perfect, the almond eyes out of a dream. Then she wrote me what has to be the most beautiful thing anyone has ever said to me: my heart takes you.

She wrote this soon after we had spoken to each other by phone transatlantically. Her years in Senegal had given her a pronounced and musical French accent. As we talked I could not get over the lovely lilt to her voice. Although we only spoke a short while, the conversation seemed to linger, like an expensive perfume. A profound shift in emotions was certainly taking place within me, something I never would have guessed could happen.

And then she wrote me those poetic words, her Sierra Leonian English filled with such unusual and quotable phrases. We fell in love. How would we ever get together?

Overnight a deep relationship developed. If you think no one can have an internet relationship with any real meaning, allow me to disagree. This internet connection took over my life. At this time I was no longer an adjunct professor teaching part-time at several different area colleges. I was full-time faculty at Mid-South Community College, a junior college located across the Mississippi River in West Memphis, Arkansas. Although my circumstances were improving, I had a lot of financial healing ahead of me.

Fatima and I had learned to save money on expensive overseas phone calls by Skyping, which was new at the time. We spoke to each other at least twice a week or more and developed a routine of daily emails. Skipping a day inevitably produced anxiety and distress and we seldom missed our appointed hours. On occasion she would Skype me using a webcam at her cyber café. Although the connections were seldom satisfying I could clearly see her great beauty and sex appeal.

A few months into our relationship, I came down with a debilitating illness people later called the 24-hour flu. Like the flu, which I've had twice in my life, it came on suddenly, without warning, and quickly put me out of commission and in my bed, barely able to get up for bathroom needs. There was no question of getting up to answer the phone or the door.

After two days and no telling how many phone calls that I didn't answer, I was finally able to get up and get a bit of food in me. The phone rang and this time I answered. It was Fatima in near hysteria.

"Why haven't you answered the phone? I've called you twenty times," she exaggerated. "What is wrong?"

When I told her I had been very sick and couldn't get up to answer the phone she broke down and bawled. There was no question that she had been worried sick, and I was deeply touched by her concern for me. It is something I would not forget, sometimes to my own detriment.

By this time I knew a lot about her, or so I thought. Because schooling in Sierra Leone is much cheaper than that in Senegal she sent her daughter Adama to live with her mother back in Freetown. Her father was deceased. One of her sisters was still living in Sierra Leone, another was in the U.S. living in New Hampshire. Two younger brothers lived in Dakar near her. There was a strange young man who Fatima claimed was like a member of the family, named Abdul as I recall. He lived in the same apartment building as Fatima and they seemed to hang around each other a lot.

Late one evening I got a phone call—from Senegal—and it was this Abdul fellow on the line. He told me that Fatima had been in a taxi with some of the girls she worked with at the beauty salon and there had been an accident. Fatima was in the hospital with a broken leg. She needed me to call her.

I dialed her number and a very different Fatima answered the phone. She sounded groggy and was barely coherent. Of course I was extremely alarmed, but there wasn't a thing I could do to help. I told her I loved her and hung up and worried. In the next few weeks Fatima said she had a "plaster" on her leg and had to walk using crutches. The way she described having to hobble to a cyber café to write me brought tears to my eyes. Then she told me she couldn't work at the beauty salon with a broken leg and be on her feet all day, and she didn't know what she would do (hint, hint).

As in love as I was, I had done my homework about relationships with foreign women. Could I trust this person completely, or was she, like so many others out there, conning me to get an American husband and an American life? I could not find much on the internet from guys who had gotten burned marrying Africans. Russians, yes. Filipinos, yes. Africans, no. I was on the alert from the very start about any requests for money. There hadn't been any. Now, there was.

So I began dribbling in payments of a few hundred dollars a month to help her out until the cast came off, money I really could not spare. By the time her leg had healed the beauty salon was closed and out of business, or so Fatima claimed, the owner having moved back to her native France. I kept up the monthly payments long after the cast came off.

The broken leg from the car crash is something that troubles me even today. Did it really happen or was this an elaborate con to get me to send money so she could live on Easy Street in Dakar? I never saw one iota of proof that her leg had ever been broken. When we finally met in Dakar six months or so later, there was no lingering limp, no pain, no mention of it. If I brought it up in conversation, the subject was usually quickly dispensed with. A broken leg from a car crash is something that doesn't heal like a scratch or a bruise. It usually takes a very long time, months, to completely mend and has lingering aftereffects. With Fatima there were none.

Exactly why Abdul called me and not one of Fatima's brothers, also disturbed me. Abdul was nowhere to be seen when I visited Dakar. Conveniently he was out of town, so it was said when I asked. In later years this tangle of unanswered questions began to loom much larger.

In Dakar, finally together.

Fatima and I had met online in June of 2003. As the months passed and our passions accelerated, the question to answer was how we could come together. Fatima was penniless and I was still recovering from divorce and my own financial setbacks. The idea was for her to come to America and live with me. But this was fantastically difficult; immigration from a third world country was no easier then than it is now. It was possible for Fatima to come to the U.S. on a student visa, but the red tape involved was Kafkaesque. To sponsor a student required a deposit of a huge sum of money, an amount far above my means. I knew of a history professor at the University of Memphis who was supposed to be an expert on Africa, and after a little digging, I further discovered that he was a white man married to a Ghanian. I felt he could offer some insight and advice for my situation.

Although I had told my mother about Fatima, and not unexpectedly gotten a negative reaction, I had told very few others. One close friend I happened to tell sniffed and told me that chasing an African woman was ridiculous and "giving in to fantasies." So I kept my secret to myself and inwardly suffered because there was no one who could sensibly advise me. This professor seemed as good as anyone to consult.

So I called and arranged for a meeting. The professor was young, full of intellectual and physical vigor, and didn't question my relationship in the least. We talked for a very long time and he filled my head with good and sensible advice. Significantly, he told me to forget the student visa and trying to bring Fatima to the U.S.

"Why can't you just go to Africa and see her there?" he

asked.

My answer was that I would have to pay for a trip to Africa then at some point turn around and pay for Fatima to fly to the U.S. Two trips instead of one to accomplish the same goal: her living with me in the U.S. He explained that I could go to Africa, document that we had been together in Dakar and gotten engaged there, then bring her over within a few months on a fiancée visa. That way I wouldn't have to put up a heavy sponsorship fee for a student visa.

"Don't you have plastic?" he asked.

I replied that I had good credit, yes.

"Well, use that and have a great time in Senegal," he said.

This made sense. He also calmed my fears about an online relationship and told me his Ghanian wife was the love of his life and made a great spouse. I left his office with many new ideas and the confidence that I could actually make this happen.

Fatima approved the new plan and was bubbling with excitement over the prospect of my coming to Africa to be with her. By this time all of her family, spread to many corners of the globe, knew of our impending engagement and were enormously pleased and accepting, unlike my family. I would come to learn that for an African woman to marry a white man was considered a great and rare coup. To be born in one of the world's poorest countries, Sierra Leone, and graduate to the world's richest, most powerful nation was to be on a tide of great fortune. And so Fatima and I began to plan.

10 Days That Shook My World

LOOKING SEVERAL MONTHS AHEAD, I thought I could fly to Dakar, Senegal in March 2004 during Spring Break, when I would not be teaching. This trip would cost several thousand dollars, no matter how pennywise I was. Yes, I could put a lot of the cost on my credit cards, but I am phobic about suffocating amounts of debt, so I decided to sell off some of my valuables to pay for the whole thing. Over the years I had accumulated some very nice electric guitars. At that time I owned six. I sold all but one including my treasured 1971 Les Paul that had been customized to get a Peter Green tone (the guitarist who founded Fleetwood Mac) and an Eric Clapton tone from his time with John Mayall's Bluesbreakers. This was one of those magic guitars; anyone who played it immediately recognized that it was a prize specimen. I sold it for high dollar on eBay to a gentleman in Perth, Australia who collected Les Pauls. It cost several hundred dollars just to ship the guitar to Perth via FedEx. When the buyer received the guitar he was so pleased with it that he emailed me photographs of the guitar on his deck, in his den, in his music room, etc. Only a guitar player will understand how someone can be so devoted to a musical instrument. I also sold my Dynaco 70 stereo amplifier, which I still miss.

I had only ever been to Canada and Mexico. I had never traveled overseas and I was anxious. Fatima had arranged a townhouse just for the two of us and I had wired her the money for a down payment for the reservation. I got my passport, I got my shots, I got my bottle of *huge* malaria pills, and I listened to the few friends who knew about my impending trip warning me to be careful about AIDS, even though Senegal has one of Africa's lowest rates of HIV infection. The day finally arrived for my flight. I did not sleep a wink the night before.

The trip took me from Memphis to New York where a freak ice storm nearly grounded all flights. As it was, it took more than an hour for the wings to be de-iced, delaying the departure time to Dakar. I am a big and tall man, and I get very anxious strapped into a confining space in a claustrophobic setting. I had been advised to take a Benadryl before boarding the plane so that I could sleep through most of the flight. It didn't work. I was way too wired to sleep and so the flight was miserable for me. Roughly eight hours later the plane kissed the tarmac at the Dakar airport, and after deplaning we had to walk at least 100 yards across the pavement and into the airport. My senses came alive in this short walk and the air itself seemed spiced. In fact, the whole time I was in Dakar the exotic smells of home fires and African cooking never left me. Something that is rarely discussed is how colors look different in the sunlight of different geographic locations. For example, to me, colors seem deep and rich in Northern countries such as Sweden. But the colors in Dakar seemed positively electric, neon, and were dazzling to behold.

It had to be me: one of my suitcases, loaded with presents and goodies from the U.S., didn't make it onto my flight from New York. So as the passengers all left, I was the remaining one having to fill out paperwork for a search for my suitcase. When I finally was able to leave the terminal I saw a door open and six or seven faces peering in from the passenger pick-up area outdoors. I immediately saw Fatima. They had been waiting on me nearly two hours. The beginning of the best ten days of my life started when I rushed out the door and picked up Fatima in my arms, kissing her in front of her friends, her brother, her cousin (the magistrate), and several others.

There were tears, there were hugs, there were handshakes, and in my life I cannot think of a more blissful moment.

Fatima's cousin—the magistrate, a top official in Dakar I would discover—had driven everyone to the airport to meet me in his shiny, black Mercedes. Fatima and I held hands and snuggled and looked into each other's eyes. I have never felt love at this level before or since.

The only thing about Fatima that was unexpected was that she was darker in person than the many pictures of her I had seen by this point. I learned that African women often used skin lightening potions that sometimes had deleterious long-term effects on their skin. Fatima normally has a café au lait complexion, but she can darken rapidly if she spends much time outdoors.

After several hours of pleasantries with family and friends, Fatima and I were finally alone together in our rented townhouse, where we made passionate, transcendent love and I marveled at her magnificent figure and lovemaking skills. Which puzzled me a bit. Fatima was a virgin when she married Alimamy Sesay, her husband who was murdered by rebels. I do not doubt this. She further told me shortly after we met online that she had only two boyfriends during her six years in Senegal. The portrait of herself that she painted was of a woman with very little worldly skills in the art of sex. But as we consummated our relationship her skill set surprised me. She knew precisely what she doing.

I was crazy in love. From a cyber café in Dakar, I mass-emailed all my friends who didn't know a thing about my relationship with Fatima and told them I was in Dakar with the love of my life. Many of them thought I was playing some kind of elaborate joke. Many more of them thought I had lost my mind. Fatima and I traveled all over Dakar during the next ten days, and I fell in love with the city just as I had with her. We ate wonderful food, had lots of fun with her friends, and to me it was euphoric. I had to call my Mom to let her know I was safe and sound. I joked with Fatima's friends that my Mom thought they might put me in a big cooking pot and boil me and eat me. They thought that was the funniest thing ever. Another thing I did before I left the States was buy several packages of Pop Rocks, that candy that pops and tingles in your mouth. I passed these around without explaining what they were and as our guests tried it the expressions on their faces when the Pop Rocks did their business is something that makes me laugh even now. My soon to be brother-in-law, Mustapha, was equally enthralled with the Listerine breath strips I had brought. He took a packet without our knowledge; he couldn't wait to try them out on his friends.

My most Hemingway moment occurred later that week. I was shaking hands in a welcoming procession for me when I was introduced to a young man named Mohammed. I reached out my hand to shake his when I noticed to my horror he had no hands. I later learned that he was a victim of the crazed rebels in the Sierra Leone civil wars.

"Do you want short sleeves or long sleeves?" the rebels would ask as they brandished their machetes. If they answered "long sleeves" their hands would be amputated. If they answered "short sleeves," their arms would be amputated. When I offered my hand, Mohammed offered his stump. As he did this he looked me directly in the eye to see if I would blanch or recoil in any way. Instead, I shook his stump just as if it were his hand, and he nodded and grinned approval. In his eye-to-eye contact what was conveyed to me was that I was a man. I didn't flinch.

Another friend of Fatima's, a girl named Fanta, lit the room like a 200-watt lightbulb. She sprang into the living room of the rented townhouse and proceeded to entertain and tell hilarious stories, many of them about Fatima. We laughed and carried on into the late night.

When she left Fatima told me, "That girl is funny but she is seriously crazy."

There was something about Fanta's body language and expressions that reminded me of black prostitutes back home in

Memphis. I didn't let on, of course.

Several days later Fatima got a phone call where she learned Fanta was in jail, having been arrested without her papers in the nightclub district in Dakar. In Dakar, families are expected to bring food for their relations who are in lock-up. Since Fanta's family was back in Sierra Leone, she desperately needed her friends to bring her food. Fatima was angry and very upset at Fanta's predicament which she blamed entirely on her friend's lack of common sense and foolishness.

Exactly why she didn't have her papers on her seemed very strange to me. And although I knew many countries were strict about having proper papers on your person at all times I couldn't help but think there was more to the story that Fatima wasn't telling me. I knew from my short time in Dakar that prostitutes paraded the nightclub district and often were arrested for solicitation. It eventually occurred to me that Fanta was doing more than partying in the nightclub district. And if she were a prostitute and a close friend of Fatima's, did that mean that Fatima might have some similar skeletons in her closet? I would never know.

No one had told me that a family elder had to approve and bless the engagement of Fatima and me. I thought that had already been decreed. However, we were required by custom to visit Fatima's paternal uncle and I had to formally request her hand in marriage. After a back-and-forth debate between family members I would ritualistically be granted permission. I was welcomed warmly to Francois Ndiaye's comfortable home. He was a math professor in one of Dakar's universities. I had sent Fatima a couple of copies of my novel

Pullers, which Francois Ndiaye happened to have in front of him. We all ate together from a large communal plate of ceebu yapp, and when we were done the formalities began.

To my deep regret, I do not speak French, the prevailing language in Dakar. Nor did Francois Ndiaye speak English. Fatima's brother Mustapha served as interpreter. As the ceremony proceeded Fatima's uncle gave several fiery speeches, very impassioned, and then he would thump his finger on my book and say *sotto voce* "Tom Graves."

I was wondering if all this fire and brimstone was a good thing, or if he thought I was some kind of white devil. I sat and listened and responded when I was asked. At one point Fatima's aunt went into a long tirade, pointing her finger at Fatima and bringing her to tears.

"Uh-oh, this thing is going sideways," I thought.

Then, unexpectedly, Mustapha looked at me and smiled.

"My uncle approves your marriage," he said.

Everyone cheered and hugged and shook hands.

Everywhere we went in Dakar when Fatima ran into someone she knew she introduced me as her husband. Not fiancé. *Husband*. There was not one hint of racial uncertainty or caution or hostility on the part of any African I met in Dakar. Everyone was perfectly lovely to me and I felt that I could spend my entire life in this beautiful city. World travelers claim that the Senegalese are the most beautiful people in the world. They most certainly are. And the bright and vibrant colors they wore accentuated their lovely dark complexions. I was bedazzled.

There were so many things to take in that week: such as

how when hailing a taxi riders hiss instead of whistling. That's right, *hiss*. How the taxi drivers can hear someone hissing with all the city clatter and noise I will never know, but I saw this with my own eyes. During Friday mid-day prayers, everyone in the city comes outdoors to pray. To be in a taxi during prayers, the muezzin singing prayers from loudspeakers rigged throughout the city, the whole population of a large city participating, is one of the most powerful sights I have ever witnessed. Fatima's brother became worried about my brazenly walking into traffic and began to hold my hand as we walked. In Senegal, men holding hands is a perfectly normal thing.

I have always been curious about African-American cultural signposts that seem to have originated in West Africa. During my time in Dakar I saw many times women carrying baskets on their heads, mostly balancing loads of laundry. This carried me into my past when it was a common sight to see black women, nearly always women, in Memphis and in the Arkansas Delta with baskets on their heads, their arms swinging freely by their sides.

The one man I remember in the fog of time who balanced something on his head was the Tomato Man walking down the middle of our street on Boyle Avenue shouting out to sell his homegrown goods. If we were playing outdoors we could hear the Tomato Man calling from blocks away. "Mighty Man," is what it sounded like he was shouting and all us kids would call back to him with a "Mighty Man" in return. We weren't mocking him, because his call and his loping presence with a basket of tomatoes balanced atop his head were fascinatingly exotic to us, something outside our everyday world and our norm.

The Tomato Man did not walk on the sidewalk, but in the middle of the street and he never went knocking door-to-door to entice people to buy his produce. It didn't dawn on me until years—decades—later that the reason he walked in the street and shouted his name the way he did was to alert housewives whose husbands were off at work during the day that he was in the neighborhood. Knocking on the doors would have likely frightened white ladies finding an imposing black man standing at their front door. In those days of open windows and fans his voice, and the children's echoes, reverberated throughout the neighborhood and the housewives wanting fresh tomatoes—and in season who didn't want some?—would come out on their front porches and wave at the Tomato Man to call him over.

I have never once seen whites balancing baskets on their heads. Which prompts me to wonder about the cultural markers that descend directly from Africa. I have always thought that many of the styles of worship in black churches, especially the Pentecostal branches of the Christian faith, derived from animist rituals in Africa. The idea of women wearing elaborate and beautiful hats in Church of God in Christ (COGIC) services strikes me as very similar to the equally elaborate head wraps of women in Nigeria. For my classes in Humanities at LeMoyne-Owen College I even show pictures of the COGIC ladies juxtaposed with African women with enormous and complicated head wraps. Most of my students think I make a valid point.

And what of James Brown? Where on Earth did he get those rituals of his where he would feign exhaustion to the point where he would be helped off-stage only to throw off his cape and rush back to his microphone, completely re-energized? The church? If so, where did the church come up with those shamanistic rituals? We all bow to Mother Africa.

The State Department strongly suggests you go to the embassy when you visit a foreign country and register with them for safety and protection. I did as I was told. Fatima and I, after showing our identification, were ushered into a waiting room and after some minutes I was called to speak to someone behind a security window.

The lady was an attractive and businesslike African-American woman who took my information, asked a few questions, and then said, "Is this woman (Fatima) with you?"

"Yes," I replied.

"You (pointing to Fatima), go sit down over there. I need to talk to him (me) alone," she said.

She then lectured me on hooking up with a Senegalese woman, how they would take your money, flim-flam you, use you to get American citizenship.

"These girls have AIDS, Mr. Graves," she sternly warned me.

Unusually, this lady gave me her personal cell phone number and told me to call her should I have any need.

Fatima is a very proud woman and was deeply insulted by the embassy official treating her so discourteously. The entire time I was in Africa I felt the attitude of superiority associated with America and being an American. It is unmistakable and very, very powerful. Several months later when Fatima got her fiancée visa to come to the U.S. she came face-to-face with this same embassy official. After examining Fatima's papers she was as polite as could be to her.

I lived a lifetime in those ten days. Nothing can dim the experience of being with Fatima in Dakar. In my life that was my mountaintop.

We were almost silent in the bumpy ride to the Dakar airport. Neither of us wanted to part. It was after midnight and the airport almost seemed deserted. Before we left, Fatima's friend Tina insisted on a prayer circle. Muslims and Christians and Tom Graves all holding hands and everyone, including me, praying out loud for my safe trip and giving thanks for our time together. It was an incandescent moment and even though I'm not a religious man I appreciated this extra dose of love and care from these people who would never again be strangers to me.

In the airport, it was time to part and Fatima grabbed me one last time and held me so tightly I could not breathe. I turned around and walked off without saying another word, and did not turn back to look at her. I knew we would both lose it if I did. Fatima went back to the townhouse and cried for hours, even unto the next day. I had left my heart behind, and I did not know how I could face the weeks and months ahead without her.

An Internal Hum

THE RACE WAS ON. I had left Dakar in the middle of March 2004 and now the pressure was building for me to bring Fatima to Memphis. I had made sure to fully document my time in Dakar with Fatima with an appropriate paper trail, photographs of us together there, and a large batch of emails proving without doubt that our relationship had developed over time. I even had proof of the wedding rings I had bought in Dakar. I conferred with immigration attorneys I knew for the best ways to get a fiancée visa quickly. There was no magic formula to move to the head of the line, but I studied and double-checked every requirement on every form and made absolutely sure there were no mistakes that would cause the visa to be rejected. I learned that very few people on their own, without attorney help, produce error-free applications.

I still sent Fatima money every month. Since her car accident, she had not worked at all. After returning to the U.S. we resumed our emails and Skype calls and occasionally we would have mild lovers' quarrels long distance. Although my funds were low, I had saved and pinched and sold off nearly every valuable I had for Fatima's upcoming trip to America. Of course the visa cost a bundle too, and it was all on me. Fatima had no money. She had never had a bank account in her life and had never written a check.

Fatima's visa was approved in September 2004. We bought a one-way ticket for her to fly to Memphis on October 1. I had already made many preparations for her. I wanted her to feel at home when she arrived, so I sought out an African market way across town that carried a few of the food items I knew she would want. I had a list that included a foreign version of Nescafé instant coffee, dried fish, cassava leaf, the type of rice she liked, and one that puzzled me called ground nut paste. No one seemed to know what ground nut paste was and it wasn't in a single foreign market I visited. When I got online to research ground nut paste I quickly discovered that this was the African name for peanut butter. While I was at the African market that day, the clerks were curious enough about a white man asking for these African foods that they had to ask why I was seeking those items. I explained that I had a fiancée coming from Senegal who was born in Sierra Leone. A clerk told me that a couple in the store was from Freetown, Sierra Leone and that I should talk to them. This was how I met a couple I will call Mr. Kalawa and his wife Salamatu. Mr. (Foday) Kalawa was a banker, with a rich, plummy accent and perfect, proper English who was obviously well-educated and with the Queen's high manners. The Kalawas were very excited by the news of my fiancée. We exchanged numbers and made many promises to get together when Fatima arrived.

Later that day when I spoke to Fatima over the phone she was boiling mad that I had given my phone number to Salamatu.

She accused Salamatu of trying to steal me away from her and told me that I was naïve not to know how Sierra Leonian women are devious—"women are the Devil," she told me—and will snatch men away from their wives and fiancées. Well, I thought this was poppycock and told her so and it was a few days before the matter finally calmed down. After Fatima arrived in Memphis I insisted that we call the Kalawas and make plans to visit with them. She very reluctantly agreed and with great apprehension we met. Salamatu and Fatima became fast friends and are still close today. Over the years we were invited to several of the Kalawas' family get-togethers and I got to know Salamatu's handsome (that's the word I would use) mother, who is the best African cook I've ever met. Her cassava leaf is in a class by itself. After our divorce, the Kalawas missed having both Fatima *and* me at their gatherings. After all, we had watched their beautiful children grow up and the Kalawas move from a black neighborhood of low pedigree to a suburban McMansion. So, for one Christmas we returned to their home as a couple again and had a delightful time. Mr. Kalawa again told me he wanted to travel with me back to Freetown, Sierra Leone. He wanted to show me his country.

I would like to share an aside about Mr. Kalawa. He came to America as a foreign exchange student in the late '70s at, of all places, Ole Miss. Probably like most whites, I had always assumed a brotherly love between Africans and African-Americans, the latter term, by the way, very frowned-on by Africans. They use the term "black Americans." They do not think African-Americans are in any way like Africans. It was the writer and critic Ed Ward who first told me of the long-simmering enmity between American blacks and Jamaicans and how when Bob Marley worked in the U.S. for a time, he didn't like American blacks at all.

When Mr. Kalawa was a student, one weekend he was driving through one of the Mississippi counties notorious for harassing blacks who were passing through. None of the Ole Miss African-Americans had warned him to stay away from that area. As could be expected he was pulled over by the law there.

"Boy, we don't take kindly to niggers we don't know coming through our part of Mississippi," the sheriff barked at Mr. Kalawa.

"Excuse me sir," Mr. Kalawa replied, "but I am not a nigger. I am an African. I am from the African country of Sierra Leone."

The sheriff was so startled by the response in that perfect high-toned accent that he immediately let him go.

Although the African-Americans at Ole Miss were polite enough to Mr. Kalawa, they still kept him at arm's length. He had more close white friends than black, which is very common with African immigrants. One Christmas he was forced to stay by himself in the men's dorms. He had nowhere to go or anyone to visit during the holidays, which made him very homesick and depressed. When the students returned from Christmas break, some of the African-American students brought Mr. Kalawa their Christmas leftovers. To an African, being offered leftovers—dog scraps—is a huge insult. He knew these students meant well, but since none of them saw fit to invite him to their homes for a Christmas dinner he threw away all the leftovers. Even today he still deeply feels the hurt of being ostracized at Ole Miss.

Fatima was due to arrive in Nashville around 10 p.m. on October 1. I drove three hours from Memphis to Nashville and with huge anticipation sat nervously and waited. And waited. And waited. Her flight had several delays and about 2 a.m. the flight finally arrived at the nearly empty airport. It seemed like 500 very tired people straggled off the plane before Fatima did, but there she was, finally. I ran to her and quickly picked her up, twirled her around, and plied her with kisses. It is hands-down one of the happiest moments of my life. Fatima was happy too, but an inner tuning fork inside me began to hum. Something wasn't right. Dare I think it? Fatima seemed a tiny bit *reluctant*. This was in no way visible; it was all completely an internal warning light, something I *felt*, I *sensed*. I chalked it up to nerves and exhaustion. I knew she was dead tired and so was I.

I thought Fatima might be so wired that we would chatter all the way back home, but she almost immediately fell asleep and slept almost the whole drive back to Memphis. I woke her up to tell her we were home and she was instantly on high alert. As I toured her through my Midtown home she literally jumped up and down as I took her from room to room. She was so pleased that she was in tears. After settling in we were both so tired that I suggested we go straightaway to bed. To my surprise she wanted me in her arms first, and we sank into bliss and love and finally to a very long and restful sleep.

The next day I drove her all over her new city and she was wowed. After dark I drove across the Mississippi River to West Memphis, Arkansas just so we could see the night skyline coming back across to Memphis.

"I have never seen anything this beautiful," she remarked.

We were getting hungry and I told her, "I guess it's time you were introduced to McDonald's."

I went to the drive-through speaker and when the voice came over the loudspeaker to take our order Fatima began looking this way and that, searching for the source of the disembodied voice.

"Where is she?" she wanted to know.

I began to laugh, further puzzling her. I had to explain in detail how the system worked. It was a very long time before Fatima understood that at fast-food places like McDonald's you couldn't customize your burger or mix and match combo meals. It took her months to learn that a Big Mac is at McDonald's and a Whopper is at Burger King. Even today she can take a ridiculous amount of time ordering a meal at a restaurant and often must ask numerous questions of the wait staff before making up her mind.

My family made it clear that they thought I was out of my ever-loving noggin wanting to marry an African woman. Racism reared its ugly head. A little more than a week after Fatima came to Memphis, my Mom called me on my cell phone right when I was close by her house, which was in the suburbs. She wanted me to pick something up from her and I told her that I was just blocks away and that Fatima was with me.

She told me, "Well, I'll have to meet her sooner or later, so just come on."

Mom and my step-father Walter weren't expecting what

walked in the door—a very tall and very beautiful African woman who didn't look anything like the Memphis blacks they were used to. When they heard her speak in her mellifluous French accent, I could see their caution melt away. Fatima called my mother "Mama Sue," and ever-after she loved being called that. I knew that Fatima had won them both over when Mom suggested we all go out to dinner and they insisted on paying.

Fatima stayed so close to me, holding my hand, snuggling close, walking arm-in-arm that Mom and Walter could see we were deeply in love. And that is how Fatima charmed them. Soon after, my daughter Marie met us for brunch at a local restaurant. When Fatima swanned into the room and held out her arms to hug her, Marie was likewise dazzled.

"My God, Fatima! You are beautiful! Way to go Dad!" she said.

Everyone who had objected to my relationship with an African woman were bowled over when they met Fatima. She charmed them one and all.

In the next few weeks that internal tuning fork that warned me something was wrong began to hum louder and louder.

The Worst Day of My Life

IF I AM EVER asked what the worst day of my life was, I don't even have to think about it. It was near the end of October, only weeks after Fatima had arrived in Memphis. I woke up one weekday morning and just as had happened with my black girlfriend Lisa a couple of years earlier, Fatima was awake next to me in bed and staring straight into my eyes. As I came out of the fog of sleep I could see by her expression that something was dreadfully wrong. As soon as she could see that I was awake she began to cry and wail. I had never seen her like this in the short time I had been with her.

She got out of bed and began to pace and wail, saying "Oh my God!" over and over.

"What's the matter?" I repeated several times before she could answer.

"My husband came to me in a vision and told me that I was his and could not be yours. He said I would always be his and his alone. He told me he had *pregnanted* me and I would have his child."

I laughed softly and said, "Honey, you've just had a bad dream. That's all. None of this is real."

"No," she implored me. "You don't believe in these things but in Africa we do. This was not a dream. I saw him. It was a vision. I never told you but sometimes I see him in places. I can be walking and see him in a crowd looking at me. Sometimes he says things to me. And women in Africa can get *pregnanted* from visions and from ghosts."

"Well, in America we don't believe in this kind of nonsense, so you just need to tell yourself that you had a bad dream and that there is no way you can be pregnant. As you know I had a vasectomy and I can't get you pregnant. So, just try to forget all this."

She was still distraught and I had to go to teach at the community college in West Memphis, so I told her to just stay home from working at the braiding salon that day and I'd be back and we would talk about it.

With Fatima still tearfully wringing her hands, I left for work. In mid-afternoon I was done at school and prepared to head back home. I had an idea to calm Fatima down and stopped at a nearby Walgreen's to pick up a pregnancy test kit. When I got home she was still highly agitated. I showed her the pregnancy kit and told her all she needed to do was pee on the stick and she would see how foolish and silly it was thinking she might be pregnant. She did as instructed and a few minutes later came out of the bathroom and handed me the stick. I was laughing and joking about the whole thing until the positive symbol became clearly visible on the stick.

When I said almost to myself, "My God, this thing says you're pregnant!" Fatima screamed and became hysterical.

I said out loud, "How in the world can you be pregnant?"

She ran into the kitchen and took out the biggest knife from the knife block and threatened to cut "it" out of her stomach.

There were many firsts for me with Fatima. Trying to talk a crazed African from cutting her own belly with a razor sharp chef knife to kill the fetus inside her was a first I had never reckoned on. I was totally afraid she would do it. I did everything I could think of to talk her out of cutting herself. I finally took the knife from her hand and put the knives up in the closet where she couldn't easily get them. She was shaking and talking so crazy at this point that the only thing I could think to do was take her to the emergency room.

On the way I looked into her eyes and said, "Fatima, tell me the truth. Have you been with anyone else besides me?"

"No," she said. "If I'm pregnant then your operation didn't work. It's your baby."

"I don't think so," I said softly.

When we got to the emergency room Fatima was shaking as if she were freezing and almost catatonic. I explained what had happened to the emergency room personnel and they suggested a better pregnancy test than the ones available in drugstores. The hospital test would be definitive.

So Fatima peed in a cup, the urine was tested, and an hour later we got the results. Positive. No question about it, she was pregnant. My heart felt as if it had been placed in a deep freeze. My emotions were numbed, Novocained.

A nurse on duty who didn't understand the gravity of the situation gave Fatima a big hug and said, "Congratulations hon', you're goin' to have a baby."

I could have killed them both.

Another nurse suggested we get an ultrasound and see how far along the baby was. As these terrible events were unfolding, my next-door neighbor and close friend, the late Doug Lowrie, a retired Memphis city cop, stumbled right into the middle of all the drama by calling me on my cell phone. In the months ahead he was the sole person who knew of my dilemma. I told no one else. Me becoming best friends with an MPD cop, on the face of it, was a highly unlikely occurrence. But our personalities clicked and we would spend long summer nights on my front porch, swatting mosquitos and swapping stories, nights I miss. He developed enough trust in me that he told me the *real* police stories, the ones I don't dare repeat even now. He convinced his cop buddies that I was okay, and they would talk freely with me present.

Doug said to me that night, "Hang in there, Tom. You *will* get through this. I'm gonna pray for you buddy."

We went to the ultrasound clinic there in the hospital and when the lady technician came in Fatima could barely answer any of her questions. I had to explain the whole predicament and the tech wound up doing all the talking to me. They got Fatima prepped for the ultrasound, squeezed a large glob of K-Y on her stomach and a few moments later I could see a tiny image of a fetus on the screen. Something inside me died then and there.

"She's seven to eight weeks now," the technician told me without even looking at Fatima, who didn't say a word.

"She's only been with me here in the U.S. for about four weeks now," I said quietly.

My eyes met the technician's and she answered a simple,

"Yeah."

I was angry, hurt, disgusted, and confused.

I told Fatima, "Get dressed and let's go."

Almost silently she got dressed, we signed some papers, and rode the elevator to the bottom floor, with neither of us speaking.

When the elevator reached the bottom floor I walked out without looking back to see if Fatima was following or not. At that moment I just didn't care. About halfway to the parking lot Fatima grabbed me and tried to kiss me. A forced kiss. I withdrew and kept walking.

"I love you. Say something, please," she begged.

I didn't feel like talking.

As I drove towards home, only a few blocks from the hospital Fatima desperately grabbed at me trying to get me to kiss her and prove I still loved her. I pushed her away. She kept coming. The next thing I knew blue lights were flashing behind me and a loudspeaker was telling me to pull over. Two o'clock in the morning, the worst day of my life, and now I had to deal with the fucking police.

When we had passed the police car, what they saw looked like a white john fighting with his black hooker, something they had seen no telling how many times. Memphis cops do not play, and they certainly weren't playing with me. They demanded to know why I was hitting this woman. I tried to explain that this was my fiancée and that she was trying to force me to kiss her. Well, that wasn't good enough for the cops. They wanted to know more. And I had to tell them the whole sordid story of how Fatima had wound up pregnant.

When they saw that she was indeed my fiancée and that she had no bruises or bleeding and that I was telling the truth they reluctantly let us go.

Back home I told Fatima to come off of it and tell me the truth. No way was this baby mine; I had a vasectomy for one thing and I had proof the baby was conceived when she was in Dakar. What happened? Who had she been with?

It took the better part of the night but the story that finally emerged was this: Fatima claimed that during her six-plus years in Dakar she had had only two lovers. She had caught her first lover with another woman and ended the relationship. He was a computer I.T. tech and got a job in France. Several months after I had met with Fatima in Dakar in March 2004, this former lover had come back for a visit in Dakar and sought out his old girlfriend, Fatima. She claimed that she told him she was engaged to me and coming to the States but that he wanted her to go shopping with him and to visit with his family.

She agreed and went off on a shopping spree with the ex-boyfriend, with him buying her lots of gifts. She claims that they went to his hotel room where there were several members of his family and that they entertained each other until later that night. After the family left and Fatima and the ex-boyfriend were alone together, she claims he locked the door and pounced on her, forcing his way with her on a sofa. When he was done and spent, she left shamed and disgusted (she said) and tried her best to forget the incident. When he came back around with flowers she claims she told others to send him away.

This was her story and over the many years to come she never wavered from it. Fatima is nearly six feet tall and very strong.

"How," I asked her, "could he hold down a strong woman like you?"

"He wasn't like you," she told me somewhat sneeringly. "He was an iron man. He worked out with weights and he was much stronger than me and you."

"So if you were engaged to me, why were you running around with an old boyfriend in the first place?"

"It was a mistake."

"And the sex happened only one time?"

"Yes."

This was the bitterest of pills to swallow. As much as I tried to believe her, in the end I just couldn't accept all the implausibilities. I remembered that fellow named Abdul and how he always seemed to be around Fatima's apartment. Many times I heard voices in the background when I was on the phone with her, male voices it seemed to me, and Fatima would say it was people on the street outside her window. On my visit to Dakar the streets at night were never that crowded and noisy. And there was the puzzle of Fatima basically raising Abdul's son along with her daughter. This whole thing just felt wrong.

Occam's Razor is a philosophical principle that posits that the simplest explanation for something is usually the correct one. Following this as a guide, the true story of Fatima's pregnancy would seem to me to be that Fatima had a boyfriend in Dakar the whole time I was engaged to her. It is highly likely he was in on the con to find a gullible American who would send her money, marry her, get her a green card, and make her an American citizen. It is possible that this boy child she raised was the product of this relationship. The fact of Fatima waking up in a hospital and finding out she was pregnant from her first husband, after they had failed to have a child during six years of marriage, seemed too much of a coincidence as well.

In my view, Fatima was lax and careless with sex with her lover. She stupidly did not check to see if she was pregnant before coming to America. Had she taken precautions and never gotten pregnant, things would have gone much differently in our marriage. Perhaps it would have even survived.

Thinking back to Abdul calling me in the middle of the night about Fatima being in a car accident seemed to me more and more of a set-up. This was a ruse to get me to send money. And it worked.

In the days that followed that terrible day, I told Fatima point blank that there was no way I was going to raise someone else's child. If she wanted to have that child, then I'd scrape together the money and send her back to Africa.

"No, I want to be with you. It was a mistake," she repeated. "I will terminate."

I told Fatima that I wanted to talk to her mother, her mother who could not speak English. I demanded that Fatima tell her mother what had happened and ask her if she wanted Fatima to stay with me or come back home to Africa.

The call was placed to Freetown, Sierra Leone and Fatima

in her mother's tongue told her what had happened with her pregnancy. Her mother became livid and raised hell with her daughter. I could hear her yelling from the phone. Eventually I was asked to speak to her mother with Fatima translating.

"Do you want Fatima back home or should I keep her here with me?"

"Please, please, I beg you to forgive her and keep her. It was a mistake. Please forgive her."

Even in Temne, her tribal language, I got her mother's message loud and clear. And the last word she said to me needed no translation:

"Terminate."

Terminate

THE CLINIC WAS TUCKED away in an odd corner of Midtown Memphis and was so anonymous that unless you knew what went on behind those doors you would never guess it was a focal point of the most bitter sides of the most bitter conflict in the city. And yet here I was, a place I'd sworn to myself I would never be. Before my first marriage my sexual experiences were so limited that I barely had to even ask about birth control or protection, yet I did. Before my first wife and I were sexually active I had dutifully inquired if she were on the pill or not and I had condoms in my wallet— didn't every hopeful young man?—just in case.

Within a few years of the birth of our daughter, Marie, my first wife Katrina was told by her gynecologist that she had been on birth control pills for a maximum amount of time and she needed to get off them. Birth control procedures, including tubal ligation, were not allowed at the Catholic hospital where Katrina worked and were not covered by her insurance. The cost outside the network being prohibitive, we turned to condoms, spermicides, and all kinds of peculiar potions on the market, none of which proved satisfactory or pleasurable. So the ultimatum came down—put up with all these prehistoric contraceptives or get a vasectomy. As rare as sex was in the Graves' household, I wanted it to at least feel good. But there was a big, *big* problem.

I am highly phobic of any invasive procedure. You wouldn't believe what I put my doctors and nurses through just to get a simple blood draw. Regular hypodermic shots aren't that bad—as long as I don't look or I'm a goner. It's not the pain, which is relatively minor. It's the idea. And vasectomies are performed while you are fully awake. You get a hypo needle right in the vas deferens of both testicles. The very thought made my testicles crawl up to my throat.

It didn't take but a few more pharmaceutically-impaired sexual outings before I decided to work up my nerve and at least talk to my urologist. My urologist was as much of a friend as a physician to me and he assured me the vasectomy would be a breeze, not to worry, and was I sure I didn't want any more children? The truth was, I did want more children, but Katrina adamantly did not. She did not want to go through the agony of pregnancy and childbirth again. So, I had little choice.

I was way beyond scared when I put on my surgery gown. Totally exposed underneath. I was shaved, disinfected, and prepped with my full package protruding through a sterile surgical sheet made of plastic. The doctor came in and in his typical boisterous voice asked how I was doing.

"Scared shitless," I told him.

"You're going to be fine," he said jovially as he prepared a large syringe to numb up my vas.

Manipulating the vas with his fingers, which was a pain in a league all its own, he stuck the needle in. Sparks and stars shot out of my groin. Then he repeated the process with the other vas. While this was going on little white meteorites were speeding across my line of vision.

"You're doing fine, Tom. Hang in there," he said as my face turned more and more ashen.

At this point I could not see anything he was doing for all the layers of drapes. But I had been the medical copywriter for Richards Medical Company, a prominent manufacturer of orthopedic and otology products, soon after my marriage to Katrina. I had been within a few feet of many major orthopedic surgeries and knew the sounds and smells of the O.R. I was well familiar with the sound an electro-cautery knife makes as it does its business: an unmistakable sizzling combined with a crackling of electricity. I also well knew the smell of burning flesh, in this case my own, from this electronic knife that now often takes the place of a scalpel. Electro-cautery knives do not actually cut through flesh; they explode it. I came very close to passing out at least ten times. The little meteorites would not fly away.

The surgery probably lasted about 20 minutes but of course seemed much longer. I was told that I would need about a week to fully recover and had already been told to wear pajama or sweat pants on my way home and for several more days. I was not to lift a thing and was instructed to be very careful in my activities.

As I hobbled home, I was still pretty numbed-up and feeling little pain. But when the Novocaine wore off, my entire lower mid-section felt as if I had been given a mule kick to the nutsack. I had some pain pills, which I eagerly took, and lay sprawled on the sofa with an ice pack placed on my groin, something that took some explaining for my daughter Marie, who as I recall was about eight years old. A hilarious coincidence, one we still laugh about, is when I was sitting on the sofa with the icepack on my genitals and we were watching television. The show *Evening Shade* starring Burt Reynolds opened with a shot of Reynolds lying on his sofa with an icepack on his groin. In the show Reynolds, just like me, had gotten a vasectomy and was recuperating, much to the amusement of the characters in that episode just as my family and friends thought my predicament amusing.

Evening Shade was so funny that evening that laughing was painful. Walking was painful. Sitting was painful. Everything was painful. The thought of hopping across a mud puddle was unthinkable. Ever after, when I hear tales of macho guys who have gotten vasectomies and went and coached junior football that same evening I know I'm listening to a round of utter bullshit. Ain't nobody doin' nothin' after no vasectomy.

Marie had a couple of girlfriends, Kirsten and Alexandra, who lived around the corner and we got to know their parents pretty well. The father was British and quite a character. His name was Tony Hicks and he gained a sort of fame in the U.K. for an anti-smoking commercial he was in. Poor fellow was dying of cancer and he said into the camera that he knew he was dying but that he knew he'd make it until his daughter could come from the U.S. to see him. The final message of the commercial was that he died before his daughter made it. It was a very powerful message and apparently got a lot of attention in the U.K. You can find it on YouTube.

On a visit to her friends' house one day, Marie told their parents that I'd had my tubes tied. Their mom fell out laughing telling me this.

The vasectomy did little to improve the sex life between me and Katrina. But after the divorce I thanked my lucky stars I'd had it done because both Lisa and Fatima told me they would have wanted to have babies with me. Had that happened my life would have never stopped being complicated.

I refused to pay for any part of an abortion.

I told Fatima, "This is your choice, not mine. I never said you had to get an abortion. All I'm saying is that if you choose to have this child, I can't raise it. It's not mine. If you want the baby, you'll have to go back to Africa or make arrangements to live somewhere else. I won't be responsible. But if you want an abortion, you'll have to save your money and pay out of your own pocket. I don't want you to ever come back on me and say I forced you to have an abortion. The decision is yours and yours alone."

She made up her mind and saved her money. In the years to come this didn't stop Fatima from trying to lay the blame for the abortion at my feet, but I nipped that in the bud.

"Nope, it was your decision, your money. I had nothing to do with that."

She said, "Well, when the time comes I will have to face God on my own for what I did."

"I guess you will," I replied.

It was up to me to find an abortion clinic, a place I tried most of my life to never think of. I fully supported a woman's right to choose and still do. I don't know how anyone can think they have a right to tell a woman what to do with her body. And in the case of incest or rape I think it is a form of torture to force a woman to give birth to that unwanted child. However, I am in agreement with Norman Mailer on the subject. Abortion is killing a child and everyone should admit it. To terminate a pregnancy is as serious a decision as one can make and it should never be made lightly. I do not think it moral for a woman who has birth control available at virtually every corner market in her city, and in many places for free, to use abortion as a birth control afterthought. I believe in sexual freedom but even more believe in sexual responsibility. I understand those religious people who believe life begins at conception because biologically it most certainly does.

I also think it is probably more moral to terminate a pregnancy than to bring a child into a hate-filled home or a world of pestilence and starvation. Sometimes, in my opinion, abortion outweighs a life of squalor. Zealots on both sides of the issue I think have done a lot of damage to the women who must face these hard choices.

We located the back parking lot of the almost invisible clinic, painted grey as I recall, on one of Memphis' less traveled streets. We had our appointment. As we walked to the back door, as we had been instructed to do, two middle-aged men near the entrance approached us quietly with religious literature. These men were not firebrands or spiteful activists. They looked at us sadly and we looked at them sadly. No one was happy.

Inside it was quiet and a handful of mostly young black women flipped through magazines waiting their turn. There was only one other couple there; how sad, I thought, that most of these women had no one with them for support during this most trying of procedures. We didn't wait long before we were ushered into a large surgical room with a surgical bench with metal stirrups and complicated-looking consoles filled with instruments. A senior-aged nurse came in and with a light smile asked pertinent questions and prepared us both for what was to come. Fatima, who was scared and as was her wont nearly silent, dressed in a surgical gown and sat on the surgical bench.

Before long a doctor came into the room, introduced himself, and explained the procedure. He was of East Indian descent and spoke in near-perfect Indian-inflected English. Like the story "Hills Like White Elephants" by Ernest Hemingway, I almost expected him to tell us "it's really not anything. It's just to let the air in." The power in Hemingway's story is in what he *doesn't* say. But in the here and now nothing was hidden.

An abortion does not take long. The preparation is more time-consuming than the procedure. It's funny; when I think back on this, in my mind I am much farther away from Fatima, the doctor, the nurse, and the whole procedure than I actually was. I was only feet away. But in my mind I see everything as if I'm at least 20 feet removed. My memory wants to be backed as far away as I can get.

The doctor inserted what appeared to be a narrow vacuum tube into Fatima's uterus and turned it on. Fatima's face winced into a mask of pain. Within 30 seconds it was over. The part to me that is vivid is of the doctor going to the sink and washing blood off his surgical gloves. This was my own personal moment of horror and it has never left me.

We left quietly and went to a nearby restaurant where we ate saying very little. In the future we seldom ever brought up the subject of the abortion. The pregnancy, yes, many times. That wouldn't go away. But the abortion is something we both preferred to forget. But forgetting an abortion is not possible. The next few months were a time of pain, chaos, and confusion. You cannot just shut off the love valve. Our intimacies were entirely unaffected by the pressures we both felt. I had until Christmas Day to decide to go through with marrying Fatima or packing her up and sending her back to Senegal. I was so hurt and angry over her pregnancy that my temper fuse was at its shortest; we squabbled furiously over the most inconsequential things.

My next-door neighbor and confidant Doug believed in Christian charity and thought I should stay with Fatima. He believed that she truly loved me—I wasn't so sure—and would devote herself even more to me if I was able to put it all behind me. This would be my personal Sophie's Choice. Keep her or send her back? When an immigrant comes to the U.S. on a fiancée visa, you are required to marry within 90 days, which is nowhere near enough time to truly get to know someone. My December deadline was like a Sword of Damocles waiting to swoop down and chop.

When you lose your trust in someone, no matter how hard your heart pulls you in the other direction you can never get that trust back. I surreptitiously added spyware to my computer that would track every keystroke made by both me and Fatima. If she had a lover back in Senegal I thought I'd find out sooner or later. Sure enough only weeks after I had installed the program, I saw a rash of emails to someone named Prince Kamara, Kamara being a very common West African surname. The emails were very cryptic and written in the Krio lingo of Sierra Leone. They weren't exactly peons to love but they suggested something more than a casual relationship.

Instead of waiting until I had further definitive proof, I angrily confronted Fatima with the emails and she went ballistic. She didn't want to address the fact of a Prince Kamara at all, but was utterly incensed that I had been spying on her, violating her privacy. I made threats in the heat of the moment, absolutely ready to get her a taxi to the airport to fly back to Africa. After hours of stalemate she came up with another of her stories; she claimed she had sensed I was spying on her and concocted an imaginary person with her sister who lived in New Hampshire. She said Prince Kamara wasn't a real person. She had her sister call me to tell me that indeed she and Fatima had planned the whole thing.

I was having a very hard time buying this story. By this time things had gotten serious enough that I had sought counseling. If you have ever been in counseling you undoubtedly know that finding the right counselor for you and your needs is of paramount importance to the success of your therapy. Many excellent counselors just may not be enough on your wave length to be effective for you. The counselor I had didn't seem to be able to wrap her head around my predicament with Fatima. When I let her read the print-out of emails to this Prince Kamara she was inclined to believe Fatima's version of events.

True enough, there was no smoking gun in those emails. Nonetheless I could smell gunsmoke. In my heart of hearts I believe Fatima had a lover in Dakar who impregnated her and this Prince Kamara likely was the man responsible. To me, with Occam's Razor to back me up, the simple version of events just made a lot more sense to me than Fatima's convoluted rationales.

I tried my very best to put it all behind me and get on with what at most times was one of the best relationships I'd ever had. I had more fun with Fatima, more laughing and joking, better sex, and an undeniable closeness than ever before. If I could just black out the dark side of Fatima, I'd have the perfect woman. I wanted to be optimistic.

But it was hard. Very hard. Fatima was highly sensitive and very high strung. She took offense easily. When angry she had a vicious tongue and when very angry would get within a fraction of an inch of my face and yell. The yin and yang of our relationship kept me mentally exhausted and on constant edge. But my counselor and my neighbor both encouraged me to go through with the marriage. As I've said, my love for her was still there. However, there were enough red flags there to think I was in a Chinese parade. I was deeply conflicted and taking things one day at a time, the only way I could cope.

One big reason I was willing to forgive Fatima and get on with the marriage is that I had my own sins to atone for. Up until the week before her arrival from Senegal, I was hitting up ladies all over town. In fact, just the week before she flew in to Nashville I had met a gorgeous light-skinned black woman at then-Memphis Mayor Willie Herenton's tailgate party and taken her home with me. I had just wrapped-up a brief affair with a black woman I had met at Wild Bill's blues club. Before this woman and I had even started seeing each other, I told her I had a woman in Africa who would be coming in October. I thought that might discourage any relationship but the woman surprised me by thanking me for my complete honesty—she said she was sick of lying dogs—and was willing to go along with my timetable.

So, I was feeling some guilt myself and not especially eager to cast stones. My counselor, a woman, was quick to remind me of my faults and failures.

Although I wanted to live with Fatima, it wasn't really my wish to ever get married again. The divorce from my first wife made me wary of going through that whole horror again. But the U.S. government gave me no alternative if I wanted Fatima in my life. I had exactly three months to marry her. That's it. Even though the pieces were by no means put back together yet, I made the decision to marry her just two days before her time was up, December 23.

Memphis has no justices of the peace. You either get married by a licensed pastor or by a judge. I tracked down a judge in Juvenile Court and we were quietly, just the two of us, married in his office. When the judge told me to kiss the bride Fatima hugged me and wept for many minutes. Later, even years later, she told me she did not think I would go through with marrying her. She was certain I was going to send her back to Africa. Wisely on my part, I had insisted on a pre-nuptial agreement drawn up by my family attorney. In case of divorce, what was mine would stay mine and what was hers—nothing—would stay hers. There would be no 50/50 split in properties. Had she refused to go along with the pre-nup, as her trouble-making sister had advised her, I would not have married her, and she was well aware that was the case.

Fatima experiencing her first snow, shortly after we wed.

We celebrated our marriage by going to a favorite restaurant, Jim's Place, which was nestled in a scenic grove of trees in the far suburbs. As we dined, something spectacular happened; it began to snow profusely, quickly blanketing the ground and surrounding trees. Fatima had never seen snow in her life and was enchanted. She believed it was a good omen for our marriage. I wanted to believe that as well, but as I would find out, it is almost impossible to right-side something thrown so topsy-turvy.

Our marriage was on crutches, and so it would stay. Fatima's temper at times bordered on violence and finally she began to get physical. During one argument she got in my face and began to push her forefinger into my forehead. I remained cool enough during that situation but warned her not to ever do that again. Some length of time later she blew up over something and picked up a nearby coffee cup and pressed it forcefully into my right cheek. It hurt. I told her quietly but with the warning abundantly clear in my voice to stop. When she kept on I lashed out with my hand and grabbed her by the throat and pushed her down into a chair. Her eyes were wide with fear.

I squeezed and said, "Goddammit I told you to stop! Now fucking stop!"

She slowly got up, went into the next room and dialed 9-1-1. I could not believe what was happening. I wasn't afraid that the police might take *me* in. We didn't speak until the doorbell rang. I answered the door, and a very young and very menacing-looking short cop stood at my door asking me what the problem was. I let him in and Fatima was practically hiding behind the living room front wall. I explained that we'd had an argument and she had pressed a coffee cup against my face. To back her off I had grabbed her by the throat and pushed her down in a chair. Other than that I'd done nothing.

He took a look at me and a look at her and said, "I can see the imprint of that cup on your face. I (talking to Fatima) don't see anything on you. You want me to run her in? (talking to me). It's obvious to me what happened."

I told him no, that I thought we had things under control.

"If I have to come back here one of you is going downtown. Do you understand me?"

We both nodded.

When the officer left she couldn't believe I'd turned the tables on her.

I said to her, "You know if they had taken me downtown and charged me with domestic abuse I probably would have lost my job? Then I would have lost my house. And where would you be? If they charged me I sure as hell would have divorced you. You don't think for shit before you do something do you? I hope to hell you learned a big lesson."

We struggled on. I never loved a woman as I did Fatima. Yet I never had the problems with a woman I did with Fatima. My neighbor Doug's prediction that Fatima would be a better wife to me because of the forgiveness in my heart was not borne out. I had read numerous complaints on the internet from men who had married foreign women and wound up supporting them as the women sent all their money back home to their families. The man's money was for both of them, but the woman's money was for her alone and it went straight back overseas.

I made it abundantly clear to Fatima that we would need to work together as a family unit to prosper and that I wouldn't put up with all her money going back to Sierra Leone. A tithe, yes, but the whole paycheck, no. I also agreed to file papers for her daughter, who at the time was about six years old, to join us in America and we would become a family. I would raise her daughter as my own.

As I write this, Fatima has yet to send for her daughter

who is now 20 years old. One of the biggest puzzles in my marriage to Fatima is why time after time she stonewalled her daughter from immigrating to, or even visiting, the U.S. She would on occasion call her daughter and on occasion send her money for birthdays and school clothes and supplies, but I never saw what I would consider a burning desire to reconnect with her only child. I have never laid eyes on Adama.

Paul Theroux in some of his travel books recounted stories of Americans who married Asian women who would wait on their husbands hand-and-foot, supplicating themselves and never leaving their side. However, once they got to the U.S. and began to see how American wives behaved, their manner changed overnight and they often turned into screaming, henpecking harpies. One story I read elsewhere about marrying Russian women really struck a nerve. The writer said that no matter how poor or how rich, Russian women were never satisfied that they had enough material possessions. If a man bought a woman a beautiful home, she would want a home even bigger, grander. If he bought her a Rolls-Royce she would want to know why he didn't buy her two. The takeaway was when the writer was asked by a friend what these women ultimately wanted. The answer was "everything."

Within a few months of Fatima's arrival in Memphis she had a closet full of new shoes. Packages would arrive from USPS, UPS, and FedEx almost daily. She had wanted a credit card—foreign women find credit cards and the ability to get it now and pay later irresistible. I full well knew the shark-infested waters of credit cards and I refused to sign her up for one. No way was I going to be on the hook for her shopping addictions. When we divorced in 2012 we had to list all our debts for the court. Fatima had 12 credit cards as I remember, most of them maxed out, and a cargo ship full of debt. I hadn't signed for a single one of those cards so I was in no way responsible or liable for the amounts owed. Even now I occasionally get a call from one of her creditors in spite of our divorce papers being signed years ago.

The one sanctuary for our marriage, where there were no problems, as I've mentioned was in the bedroom. For that I shall remain eternally grateful. There were periods where we got along fine, but something would always re-spark the buried angers. As a lover, I had no complaints with Fatima. As mentioned, she was also the funniest woman I have ever been with. We could make each other laugh (and still do) and I have never seen another woman so quick-witted. She never missed a beat. The peaks were Himalayan, the valleys Grand Canyons. Everywhere we went together people would come up to us just to see who we were. Obviously we made a scenic couple. We were both constantly amused at how little old white ladies would find an excuse to talk to Fatima. They could tell at a glance that she was different, that she wasn't a black from Memphis. They loved her accent. Fatima had been a champion track and field star in her high school days, enough so that the French Olympic team wanted her to come to France. However, her father did not want her to leave the family nest and refused. Fatima's very long legs and graceful body movements attracted everyone.

So many black men in Memphis would sidle up next to our car as we drove in the city and would make eyes at Fatima with me sitting right next to her that I had the windows tinted, which ended *that* problem. Other than that rude behavior, we never got one ounce of hostility in the city where Martin Luther King Jr. was assassinated. Only once did I see a negative reaction: a redneck-looking white lawn service guy was mowing a yard in the neighborhood behind one of those big industrial self-propelled mowers. Fatima and I were out for a walk and I noticed the guy looking at us and slowly shaking his head.

I got Fatima her first job in Memphis even before she arrived. I paid a visit to a Midtown African braiding shop and the owner—a Senegalese—told me by all means to bring her by when she arrived. And so I did and Fatima was hired on the spot. At first Fatima would give me all her money that she earned. I took a small percentage to apply towards our family bills and let her have the rest. It wasn't too long, however, before she wanted her own checking account and to maintain her own separate finances. We sat down and worked out a family budget and she paid a percentage based on her income versus mine. I paid about 75% of the bills, as I recall. Many Africans work seven days a week. Fatima wanted to do this. No matter how much I implored her, she insisted on working every day. She did not drive—teaching her to drive is something I hope to never repeat with anyone else in my lifetime— so in the first years of our marriage I was constantly having to drop her off, pick her up, worry over supper, and the strain, on top of the severe problems we were having, made me a nervous wreck.

Through a Senegalese contact she had made at the braiding salon, she got a much better job as a medical records clerk at a company that provided medical check-ups for students in the city's schools. She was very proud of her job and advanced there, eventually putting in 12 years before resigning over a trifling issue with a supervisor. Throughout the whole 12 years she continued to work every weekend at the braiding salon.

In 2010, six years after we had met on Match.com, we separated because of money. She told me she couldn't pay her share of our bills that month, even though I knew she had savings that would more than cover the amount she needed to pay. She told me she needed to send a large sum of money to her mother in Sierra Leone and would be short. This was exactly the sort of thing I had already warned her I would not tolerate, and when it comes to money Tom Graves means business. So I gave her an ultimatum—either pay your share of the bills or leave. In a great huff she packed her bags and left. Inside I felt a tremendous sigh of relief. The ten-stone weight on my back was lifted.

For the next couple of years we still saw each other frequently and were still romantic. Living apart actually improved the relationship...for a time. We still had our share of rows and soon after she returned from a two-month trip back to Sierra Leone we agreed to go on and go through with the divorce. It was not long after this that without either of us speaking of it we simply stopped any activity between the feathers. Two years ago she went for a three-month stay back in Freetown. She called and asked if I could pick her up at the airport when she returned. I did and as we were driving to her apartment I jokingly asked if she had gone and gotten married while in Freetown. She held up her hand and showed me some sparkling rings on her wedding finger.

"Yep," she said.

I thought she was joking and didn't give it a second thought.

Within a few days I saw her postings on Facebook. Wedding pictures, Fatima dressed like a bride in a Walt Disney fantasy. I was incredulous. I felt a spear go straight through my heart. My hurt after all this time we had been separated surprised me. I felt oddly empty for many days.

Fatima is now married to Ishmail Kamara, who she claims is the Customs chief at the Sierra Leone-Gambian border, which means he oversees a lot of money. I wish them well. As I write this Fatima resigned her job in Memphis, has been in Freetown for months, and is due back in Memphis within a few weeks. She says she will be moving to New Haven, Connecticut after her return. (Update: She did in fact move to New Haven. On rare occasion I hear from her.) (Update number two: She confided in me that her marriage had not worked out and she would be filing for a divorce from Mr. Kamara.)

I do not regret my marriage to Fatima or my time in Africa. I still consider my ten days in Dakar the greatest ten days of my life. However, it is not a safari I wish to re-explore. Fatima's African friends in Memphis have all dropped me. Just like that. I have made some new friends in Botswana and plan to visit there some day. I also hope to teach in Swaziland. It is possible I may teach on a Fulbright in Freetown, Sierra Leone. Now *that* would be interesting.

Fatima's daughter as I write this has still not set foot in the U.S.A.

The sad truth is, despite it all, I still love her.
And I will never know if she truly loved me.

The End

Photo Credits

Tom Graves was born in Memphis and attended Bethel Grove grammar school and graduated from Sheffield High School. He earned a B.A. in Journalism from Memphis State University and in his mid-forties earned an M.F.A. in Creative Writing from the University of Memphis. He has published six books including the award-winning *Crossroads: The Life and Afterlife of Blues Legend Robert Johnson* which has been published in four languages. He was Consulting Producer and Writer for the Emmy-winning documentary film *Best of Enemies* about the acrimonious 1968 debates between Gore Vidal and William F. Buckley Jr., a subject that had fascinated him as a freshman college student. He is a tenured English professor at LeMoyne-Owen College in Memphis, a historically black college founded after the Civil War. He is a partner with Darrin Devault in The Devault-Graves Agency, an independent publishing company.

Other Books <u>From</u> Devault-Graves Digital Editions You Will Enjoy

Crime Fiction from Chalk Line Books

A Bad Woman by James M. Cain
Sharecropper Hell by Jim Thompson
Murder At The Bijou by Jim Thomson
The Secret Squad by David Goodis
The Killing by Lionel White

Audiobooks from Devault-Graves Digital Editions

Big Sur by Jack Kerouac, read by David Angelo
Maggie Cassidy by Jack Kerouac, read by Mike Dennis
Tristessa by Jack Kerouac, read by Mike Dennis
Three Early Stories by J.D. Salinger, read by Mike Dennis
Crossroads: The Life and Afterlife of Blues Legend Robert Johnson
by Tom Graves, read by Tom Graves
Aesop's Fables with Colin Hay by Tom Graves, read by Colin Hay
Penrod by Booth Tarkington, read by Tony Scheinman
Weegee: The Autobiography by Weegee, read by Clay Lomakayu
A Bad Woman by James M. Cain, read by Mike Dennis
The Killing by Lionel White, read by Mike Dennis
Murder at the Bijou by Jim Thompson, read by Mike Dennis
Sharecropper Hell by Jim Thompson, read by Mike Dennis
The Secret Squad by David Goodis, read by Mike Dennis

**DEVAULT-GRAVES
DIGITAL EDITIONS**
www.devault-gravesagency.com